MEN-AT-ARMS SERIE

EDITOR: MARTIN WINDR

Dutch-Belgian Troops of the Napoleonic Wars

Text *by* OTTO VON PIVKA

Colour plates by CHRIS WARNER

OSPREY PUBLISHING LONDON

Published in 1980 by
Osprey Publishing Ltd
Member company of the George Philip Group
12–14 Long Acre, London WC2E 9LP
© Copyright 1980 Osprey Publishing Ltd

ISBN 0 85045 347 x

Filmset in Great Britain
Printed in Hong Kong

Author's acknowledgements
My thanks are due to the following:
Herr Schnieidereit and members of the KLIO
Arbeitsgruppe Waterloo in Düsseldorf; and, in
particular, the Historical Section of the Netherlands
Army Staff in s'Gravenhage. The Legermuseum at
Leiden is recommended for those who wish to study
this army further. Sources used in the preparation
of this book are:
    Lienhart & Humbert, *Les Uniformes de l'Armée
        Français depuis 1619 à nos Jours*, Leipzig, 1895
    Knötel, R., *Handbuchder Uniformkunde*, Hamburg,
        1937
    Suhr, C., *Die Uniformen aller in Hamburg zwischen
        1806–1813 gewesnen Truppen*
    Teupken, T. F., *Kleedingen Wapenrustingvande
        Koniklijke Nederlandsche Troepen*, s'Gravenhage
        and Amsterdam, 1823
    Documents provided by the Historical Section,
        Netherlands Army Staff.

Historical Synopsis

The Netherlands (or the Low Countries) have been for centuries the arena in which contending European powers sought to achieve martial decisions, however remote this theatre of war may have been from their homelands. The area has had a very colourful history, and in the period leading up to the Napoleonic era modern Holland was the Spanish Netherlands, Belgium the Austrian Netherlands. This connection with the North Sea gave Austria a navy 'by proxy' before she had one of her own on the Adriatic.

In 1794 France overran the Austrian Netherlands, and these provinces remained part of France until 1815. That same year, the French general Pichegru invaded the Spanish Netherlands, and founded the Batavian Republic under French protection. This caused the Prince of Orange (then ruler) to flee to England on 18 January 1795. In the ensuing Treaty of the Hague, the Dutch States General ceded to France the provinces of Flanders, Maastricht, Venlo and part of Walcheren with Flushing. In 1803 Jan Rudiger Schimmelpenninck was elected president of the Batavian Republic with the title 'Raadspensionaris' (Pensioner of the Council); the Republic now consisted of the Departments of the Ems, Old Issel, Rhein (called North Brabant in 1814), Texel, Delft, Scheldt and Maas (called Seeland in 1814) and Dommel (called North Brabant in 1814).

In 1806 this Republic was elevated to the status of the Kingdom of Holland, with Napoleon's brother Louis (called Ludwig by the Dutch) as its ruler. It was only to exist for four short years, however, before vanishing from the map of Europe. During this time Napoleon had been trying to destroy Great Britain by commercial means, as his navy had been unable to achieve anything at all against his arch-enemy. He instituted the Continental System, which involved a total embargo throughout mainland Europe on British goods, or any other trading contact with British subjects, This ruined the trade of all the European countries under his rule, France included, and all those lands having access to the

Sapeur, 7th Infantry Regiment. The bearskin has red cords and plume and brass chinscales; the yellow coat has white collar, cuffs (?), lapels and turnbacks, yellow buttons, red epaulettes, arm badges, turnback grenades and fist-strap. The gaiter buttons are white. (Plate from Otto Helms Collection, Staatsarchiv, Hamburg)

Heavy Dragoons. It will be noticed that there are no front badges on the plain brass helmets, contrasting with another Suhr plate reproduced on a later page. Dark blue coat faced red, with white buttons. Red plume; dark blue trousers with red piping, white buttons and black leather reinforcement. (This, and all the other contemporary plates used in this book but not individually credited, are from the C. Suhr collection in the Staatsarchiv, Hamburg.)

open sea became hives of smuggling. By 1810 Napoleon was so desperate to stop this traffic that he absorbed Holland, parts of Westfalia, the Duchy of Oldenburg and the Hanseatic towns of Hamburg, Bremen and Lübeck into Metropolitan France, so that he might exercise effective control over their coastlines.

When the Kingdom of Holland was thus integrated on 9 July 1810, its civil administration was modified, and on 1 January 1811 new Departments were announced. These were Zuydersee (the old Amstelland and Utrecht), Maas Estuary (the old Maasland), Scheldt Estuary (the old island of Walcheren, South and North Beveland, Schouwen and Tholen), Rhine Estuary (the old Waal, the Donge and areas of the Nethen, the lower Maas and the Roer rivers), Upper Yssel (most of the old province of Geldern), Yssel Estuary (the old Upper Yssel), Friesland, West Ems (the old Groningen, Drenthe and Riederland) and East Ems (formerly East Friesland). These Departments formed two new military divisions—the 17th, with its capital in Amsterdam, and the 31st with its capital in Groningen. (The Dutch army in July 1810 contained 19,529 Dutchmen, 1,687 French, 5,481 Germans, 15 Russians and 335 Poles, a total of 27,047 men.) When reconstructed as an independent state in 1814, these provinces were joined with parts of the old Austrian Netherlands (Belgium): the Departments of West Flanders, East Flanders, South Brabant, Limburg, Hennegau, Liège, Namur and the Grand Duchy of Luxembourg.

The armies raised from these areas fought as allies of the French (or as part of France itself) from 1795 to 1813; indeed, Holland had fought Great Britain repeatedly in earlier times, although mainly on the high seas during the great scramble of the European nations for colonies and for the world's trade. As with the armies of most other allies of France, tactics, organization, drill, weapons, equipment, badges of rank and discipline were all closely modelled on French practice, and represented an improvement on what had existed previously.

By 1814 the 'Low Countries' had thus been under Napoleonic influence for almost twenty years, and it is scarcely surprising that many old soldiers took the field in the Hundred Days nominally on the Allied side, but with very mixed feelings and confused loyalties.

Kurassiers of the 1st and 2nd Regiments in the old and new uniform, 1805. Three figures wear light blue facings (2nd Regt.) and of these the central soldier wears the new uniform of French-style cuirassier helmet, steel with a brass combe, chinscales and peak edging, red plume and black crest. His waistcoat and breeches are white, his epaulettes red and his leatherwork buff. His companions all wear the British-style 'Tarleton' helmet with red turban, steel chains and scales. Their coats still carry the lace decoration which, together with the Tarleton, should have been replaced in 1805. The left-hand man is from an élite company (red epaulettes, brass grenade on pouch, red grenades on the turnbacks). He wears grey overalls with white buttons and vandyked black leather reinforcement. The turnbacks of the right-hand man, and of the figure of the 1st Regt. trooper second from left, are red. The 1st Regt. figure has black facings and buff waistcoat, breeches and leatherwork.

In British accounts of the Waterloo campaign there have been various rather scathing accounts of the performance of the Dutch-Belgian troops present. Friction between allies is as old as history itself; chauvinism may have to be tolerated in time of national emergency, but more balanced views can prevail once the tensions have subsided. Deeper study of good sources will soon reveal that these Allied units suffered casualties no lower than those of many British regiments in these battles, and that there is considerable doubt as to the identity of one or two of the most notorious cavalry units (which could well have been volunteer or militia units and not regular army formations). Such confusion of identity will be readily understood by anyone conversant with the 'fog of war'. Perhaps it should be a lesson to us all to check and double-check our facts before publishing sweeping condemnations.

Belgian units in the French Army

Although Belgium was absorbed by France in 1794–95, it is possible to trace many of the units of the French army which were raised in that area prior to the union or recruited in it from 1794 to 1814:

French Unit	Raised	Belgian Volunteer Predecessors
15e Léger	9 February 1795	Batavian Legion
18e Léger	July 1801	North Frankish Legion
28e Léger	1 July 1793	Namur Battalion
30e Léger	11 November 1793	Infantry of the Legion Franche Etranger
55e Léger	July 1801	North Frankish Legion
22e Chasseurs	17 June 1793	Infantry of the Legion Allemande
11e Hussards	17 June 1793	Cavalry of the Legion Allemande
13e Chasseurs à Cheval	11 November 1793	cavalry of Legion Franche Etranger
14e Chasseurs à Cheval	?	Brussels Dragoons
17e Chasseurs à Cheval	?	Chevau-Légers of West Flanders
18e Chasseurs à Cheval	9 May 1793	From 14e Chasseurs à Cheval (see above)
27e Chasseurs à Cheval	29 May 1808	Liège Volunteer Cavalry

Although Belgium had no separate identity from 1794 onwards, the Spanish Netherlands became the Batavian Republic and it is her army that we shall study in closer detail.

The Batavian Republic, 1795-1806

Batavian Half-Brigade Organization, 1795

The organization of the Batavian Half-Brigades in 1795 was very much on the French model: 1 Chef de Brigade, 3 Bataillon Chefs, 2 Quartier-Maîtres, 3 Adjutant majors, 3 Chirurgiens (surgeons), 3 Adjutant sous-officers, 1 Tambour Major (drum-major), 1 Bataillons Tambour, 8 musicians, 3 tailors and 3 cobblers.

Each of the three battalions had nine companies (one grenadier and eight fusilier). A grenadier company consisted of 1 captain, 1 lieutenant, 1 sous-lieutenant, 1 sergeant-major, 2 sergeants, 1 corporal quartermaster (fourrier), 4 corporals, 4 lance-corporals, 48 grenadiers and 2 drummers—total, 65 men. A fusilier company was the same except that it had 6 corporals, 6 lance-corporals and 67 fusiliers—total, 89 men.

Each half-brigade had six 4pdr. cannon served by a company of 67 men (these pieces were withdrawn from service on 24 January 1798), and a half-brigade thus had an establishment of 2,347 men.

Uniforms
General Notes—Infantry
The uniforms had a strong French flavour, and consisted in 1795 of a plain bicorn with black cockade, white loop and button; a long, dark blue coat with facings as shown below; white belts, waistcoat, buttons and breeches, and long black gaiters. Badges of rank and company distinctions were as in France, i.e. grenadiers had red plumes, red fringed epaulettes and red sabre knots; voltigeurs had these items in green; and fusiliers had no epaulettes or sabres, and only a company pompon. Officers wore red, white and blue waist sashes and had silver sword knots.

Dutch artillery officers, Hamburg, 1805. Here the uniform colouring is the almost universal pattern of the day—dark blue with red facings and piping, and gold buttons and epaulettes. Black cockades, red plumes with black tips. While the left-hand figure has epaulettes and long coat-tails, the right-hand man has red hat tassels, no epaulettes, short tails with red grenades, and no visible marks of rank. His overalls are grey with grey-covered buttons.

The French-style system of rank badges was as follows in 1806:

Generals:
Large cocked hat with cut white feather edging; gold lace edging, loop and button; blue within white within red cockade (replaced in mid-1795 by the black cockade); gold hat tassels in the corners. Dark blue double-breasted coat with red collar and cuffs for parades, blue for daily wear; gold buttons; gold embroidery around collar, cuffs and horizontal pocket flaps—single for Generals de Brigade, double for Generals de Division; gold epaulettes with heavy bullion fringes bearing two five-pointed stars for a General de Brigade, three for a General de Division, crossed batons within a ring of silver stars for a Marshal. White waistcoat and breeches; high black boots, buckle-on steel spurs. Badge of office was a wide silk waist sash striped with gold and having gold tassels tied on the left side. Colouring was according to rank: Marshal—white, General de Division —red, General de Brigade—light blue.

Commissioned Officers:
Colonel Bicorn; two gold/silver epaulettes with heavy bullion fringes; silver portepée. Red, white and blue waist sash.
Major Shako with gold/silver top band, side chevrons and cords; two epaulettes in gold/silver with fringes in the reversed colours; silver portepée; sash as above.
Chef de Bataillon As for Colonel, but with a shako as for Major and only the left epaulette fringed.
Captain As above, but with thin epaulette fringes.
Adjutant Major As for Captain but only the right epaulette fringed.
Lieutenant As for Captain, but with single red line along epaulette straps.
Sub-Lieutenant As for Lieutenant, but with two red lines along epaulette straps.
Adjutant As for Sub-Lieutenant, but with two white/yellow lines across the epaulette strap and the epaulette fringes mixed with red.

Officers of hussars and Chasseurs à Cheval did not wear epaulettes, but their ranks were indicated by numbers of gold/silver chevrons above the pointed cuffs and around the elaborate thigh knots on the Hungarian breeches.

Non-commissioned Ranks:
Sergeant/Maréchal-des-logis chef Red and gold/silver (button colour) mixed shako cords and epaulette fringes; two gold/silver diagonal bars on the lower sleeves on red backing. In units with Polish (pointed) cuffs these bars were replaced by chevrons, point up.
Maréchal-des-logis As above but only one gold/silver bar on lower sleeves.
Fourrier One gold bar on the upper left arm; two red bars on orange backing on the lower sleeves.
Corporal Two red bars on orange backing on the lower sleeves.

Years of service were indicated by red chevrons, point up, on the left upper arm, one for each period of eight years.

In 1803–05 the Half-Brigades were split up into twenty-one individual battalions; their facings are shown in Table A. Some of the details of uniform facings were changed in certain battalions in 1804; these changes are listed in Table B.

Batavian Infantry Colour, Model 1795. Obverse: White ground, gold inscription, green oak wreath, grey cloud, steel armour and sabre blade with gold hilt and trim. Gilt pike tip; brown pike; cords and tassels of red, silver and blue. These colours were painted on silk, and 21 were presented to the 1st to 7th Half-Brigades. (After documents provided courtesy of Dutch Army Historical Section)

Batavian Infantry Facings 1795–1803

Native Units	Collar, lapels, cuffs and cuff flaps	Turnbacks	Piping
1st Half-Brigade	Red	Red	White
2nd Half-Brigade	Crimson	White	White
3rd Half-Brigade	White	White	White
4th Half-Brigade	White (red collar piped white)	Red	Red
5th Half-Brigade	Yellow	Yellow	White
6th Half-Brigade	Light blue	White	White
7th Half-Brigade	Yellow	Yellow	White
Foreign Regiments in Batavian service			
Waldeck	Yellow	Yellow	Yellow
Sachsen-Gotha	Red	Red	Red

Table A: Batavian Infantry Facings 1803–06

Battalion	Lapels and cuffs	Collar and cuff flaps	Lining	Piping to coat, lapels and cuffs	Piping to collar and cuff flaps	Colour of turnback numbers
1	red	red	red	white	white	white
2	red	dark blue	red	white	white	white
3	red	white	red	white	red	white
4	crimson	crimson	white	white	white	dark blue
5	crimson	white	white	white	crimson	dark blue
6	crimson	dark blue	white	white	white	dark blue
7	white	white	white	white	white	dark blue
8	white	dark blue	white	white	white	dark blue
9	white	red	white	white	white	dark blue
10	white	red	red	red	white	white
11	white	dark blue	red	red	white	white
12	white	white	red	red	red	white
13	light blue	light blue	light blue	white	white	white
14	light blue	dark blue	light blue	white	white	white
15	light blue	white	light blue	white	light blue	white
16	light blue	light blue	white	white	white	dark blue
17	light blue	dark blue	white	white	white	dark blue
18	light blue	red	white	white	white	dark blue
19	yellow	yellow	yellow	white	white	dark blue
20	yellow	red	yellow	white	white	dark blue
21	yellow	dark blue	yellow	white	white	dark blue
Waldeck (1st & 2nd)	yellow	yellow	yellow	yellow	yellow	none
Sachsen-Gotha	red	red	red	none	none	none

On the skirt turnbacks were worn the battalion numbers; for Battalions 1–9 they were worn on one skirt turnback with a disc in the same colour on the other; Battalions 10–21 wore the digits one on each side of each skirt turnback.

Table B: Uniform Changes of 1804

Battalion	Date	Items Changed
1	4 September	Collar and cuff flaps became red.
3	9 August	Collar, cuff flaps, lapels, turnback numbers and cuffs became light blue; piping to lapels and cuffs became red.
5	9 August	Collar and cuff flaps became crimson with white piping.
6	13 July	Lapels and cuffs became pink, collar and cuff flaps buff.
8	17 January	Collar, lapels and cuffs became red; cuff flaps remained dark blue; all piping, red.
10	29 June	Collar, lapels and cuffs became yellow, the first with white piping, the rest with red.
10	23 August	Lining changed to white; turnback numerals to dark blue.
11	27 April	Collar, lapels and cuffs became yellow without piping.
12	13 July	Collar, lapels, cuffs and lining became orange without piping; turnbacks and pocket flaps piped orange.
14	5 October	Collar, cuff flaps and all piping became light blue.
15	12 September	Cuff flaps became light blue; light blue piping to collar.
17	31 July	Collar and cuff flaps became light blue.
18	21 April	Cuff flaps became light blue.
19	31 July	All piping became yellow.

In 1805 a battalion of Grenadiers of the Guard of the Council was raised, and in 1806 it was expanded into a regiment. It wore bearskins; white coats with crimson facings; red epaulettes, plumes and sabre knots; white waistcoats, breeches and belts; black gaiters and shoes.

Jagers

These troops dressed as for the Line except that they wore dark green coats, lapels, waistcoats and breeches, dark green feather plumes, black belts (some sources show white), dark green fringed epaulettes and turnbacks. Facings were shown on collar, cuffs, cuff flaps, and piping to waistcoat and turnbacks. On the turnbacks were hunting horns in the facing colour:

	Facings	Buttons	Remarks
1st Bn.	Red	Yellow	—
2nd Bn.	Black	White	Lapels also black
3rd Bn.	Black	Yellow	Lapels dark green
4th Bn.	Crimson	White	—

In 1805 the 1st and 2nd Battalions became the 1st Light Infantry Regiment, with yellow facings, and the 3rd and 4th Battalions became the 2nd Light Infantry Regiment, with light blue facings.

General Notes—Batavian Cavalry 1795

All regiments wore a large plain bicorn with white plume, black cockade, white loop and button,

This undated Suhr plate would appear to show a corporal of the then-1st Dragoons in about 1805. On 7 September 1806 they became the 3rd Hussars, amalgamating with the 1st Hussars in 1809. Brass helmet with brass chinscales, red plume, black fur turban apparently bearing a brass lion-mask insignia. Coat, breeches, greatcoat and saddle furniture are dark blue, facings are red, and buttons are white. The shabraque is trimmed white and red and the rolled cloak on the portmanteau is red.

Sharpshooters of the 2nd, 3rd and 4th Regts., 1807–10. From left to right: *Voltigeur, 2nd Regt.* Old dark blue uniform with red facings; yellow collar showing voltigeur status; green epaulettes; green pompon, white hat loop; white belts, gaiters and smallclothes. *Voltigeur, 3rd Regt.* New white uniform with red facings, white buttons; green fringed epaulettes, not visible here; green pompon, white '3' and cords to shako—other furniture white, as 4th Regt. figure below. *Voltigeur, 2nd Regt. (rear view)* As first figure; note red turnbacks with dark blue hearts, the latter being shown in white in one copy of Suhr's work. *Voltigeur, 4th Regt.* New white uniform with pink facings, white collar piped pink (a distinction introduced on 1 March 1807 for voltigeurs of all line infantry regiments). Green pompon and fringed epaulettes; all other shako furniture white. *Voltigeur, 4th Regt. (rear view)* New uniform with old bicorne, green pompon. White hearts on long white turnbacks are possibly an oversight by the artist. Green fist-strap. *Voltigeur, 3rd Regt.* New uniform, as for second figure, but with inexplicable red shako cords. *Voltigeur, 3rd Regt.* Old uniform—dark blue coat and collar, white lapels, cuffs, cuff-flaps, turnbacks and buttons, green pompon and epaulettes.

and tricolour tassels (red, white and blue); a long-tailed white coat with facings shown on collar, lapels, cuffs and turnbacks, and fringed epaulettes; white belts, waistcoat, breeches and buttons; high-cuffed boots; a brass-hilted, straight-bladed sword in a brown leather sheath. The Dragoons' coats were dark blue.

Unit	Cuffs, collar, lapels and epaulettes	Turnbacks	Saddle furniture (edged white)
1st Heavy Cavalry	Black	Crimson	Crimson
2nd Heavy Cavalry	Light blue	Light blue	Yellow
Dragoons	Pink	Pink	Dark blue

The Hussar Regiment wore shakos, blue dolman and breeches, red collar and cuffs, yellow buttons and lace, crimson and white sash.

In 1803 the 1st and 2nd Heavy Cavalry Regiments were converted to the 1st and 2nd Light Dragoons respectively, and received new uniforms including British-style Tarleton helmets having a black fur crest, red turban and white plume. They wore short, white coats with facings shown on collar, lapels, cuffs and turnbacks. Belts, waistcoats and breeches remained white, but the heavy boots were replaced by short, hussar-type footwear often worn with grey, buttoned overalls. Saddle furniture was unchanged. Facings were black for the 1st Regiment, light blue for the 2nd.

The Tarleton helmets were replaced by brass French dragoon helmets in 1804, and in that year white lace loops were added to the collar (two each side), cuffs (two) and lapels (eight).

In 1805 the old Dragoons became the 1st Light Dragoons, the old 1st Light Dragoons became the 2nd Light Dragoons, and the old 2nd Light Dragoons was disbanded. A new unit, the 'Dragoons of the Guard' was raised in June 1805 and wore bearskins, white tunics with crimson facings and yellow lace and buttons, and brass shoulder-scales. In June 1805 the 'Guard Hussars' were raised; they wore shakos, red dolman and breeches, white pelisse, yellow lace and buttons, black fur trim, white belts, black leather sabretache, and blue and white barrel sash.

Foot Artillery 1795–1806
Infantry-style uniform, dark blue with red facings and yellow buttons, and white belts, waistcoats and breeches.
Horse Artillery 1795–1806
Dragoon-style uniform with large bicorn; dark blue coat and lapels; red collar, cuffs and turnbacks; yellow buttons; buff leather trousers, high-cuffed boots and white belts.
Engineers
As for foot artillery, but with white buttons.

Orders of Battle, 1795-1806

7 September 1796—The campaign in Germany
Batavian Division General Beurnonville
1st Brigade Lt.-Gen. H. W. Daendels
3rd Battalions of the 1st, 4th and 6th Half-Brigades, the 2nd Half-Brigade (three battalions) and the 1st and 2nd Heavy Cavalry Regiments (two squadrons each).
2nd Brigade Maj.-Gen. D. van Guericke
5th Half-Brigade (three battalions); 1st, 2nd and 3rd Jäger battalions; two squadrons of hussars and four of dragoons.
The artillery consisted of the 1st and 2nd Horse Artillery Companies.

21 March 1797—The abortive landing in Ireland:
Batavian Division Lt.-Gen. H. W. Daendels
1st, 2nd, 4th and 5th Half-Brigades (three battalions each); 3rd Battalion, 3rd Half-Brigade; 6th and 7th Half-Brigades (three battalions each); 1st-4th Jäger Battalions; 1st and 2nd Heavy Cavalry Regiments, hussars and dragoons (each of two squadrons); 1st and 2nd Companies, Horse Artillery.

Winter campaign on the River Main with General Augereau, 1800–01:
Batavian Division Lt.-Gen. Jean Baptiste Dumonceau
1st Brigade Maj.-Gen. Stuart John Bruce
1st and 2nd Bns., 1st Half-Brigade; 1st, 2nd and

3rd Bns., 2nd Half-Brigade; 3rd Bn., 3rd Half-Brigade.

1st Heavy Cavalry Regiment (two squadrons), dragoons (two squadrons).

2nd Brigade Col. C. L. Crass

3rd Bn., 4th Half-Brigade; 2nd and 3rd Bns., 5th Half-Brigade; 3rd Bn., 6th Half-Brigade; 4th Jager Bn.

Hussars (two squadrons).

1st Horse Artillery Company.

Three foot artillery companies.

Expedition to Hanover under General Bessoles, 6 June 1803:

Batavian Mobile Corps Maj.-Gen. S. J. Bruce

1st, 2nd and 3rd Bns., 5th Half-Brigade; 1st, 2nd and 3rd Bns., 6th Half-Brigade; 3rd Jager Bn. (on 23 June 1803 the 3rd Jagers were replaced by the 1st Jagers).

2nd Heavy Cavalry Regiment: dragoons.

Detachment of the 3rd Artillery Bn.

On 25 November 1803 the Corps was completely reorganized:

Batavian Infantry Colour, Model 1802. White ground, green laurel and oak sprigs, gold lion on red ground surrounded by gold riband bearing 'CONCORDIA RES PARVAE CRESCUNT'. Behind the shield a fascis and crossed sword and baton; on top of the fascis an antique helmet in silver and gold, with red, white and blue plumes; from it depend red, white and blue ribbons, with unit designation in gold at the bottom on the white stripe. (After documents provided courtesy of Dutch Army Historical Section)

Batavian Division Lt. Gen. J. B. Dumonceau

1st Brigade Maj.-Gen. C. L. Crass; *2nd Brigade* Maj.-Gen. H. von Heldring

1st Bn., 1st Half-Brigade; 2nd and 3rd Bns., 2nd Half-Brigade; 2nd Bn., 3rd Half-Brigade; 1st Bn., 4th Half-Brigade; 1st Bn., 5th Half-Brigade; 2nd and 3rd Bns., 6th Half-Brigade; 1st and 2nd Bns., 7th Half-Brigade; 2nd and 4th Jagers; 1st Bn., 1st Regiment of Waldeck; 2nd Bn., 2nd Regiment of Waldeck; Grenadier Bn. (composed of the four grenadier companies of the 1st and 2nd Waldeck Regiments and of the two grenadier companies of the Regiment Sachsen-Gotha.

Dragoons (2nd and 3rd squadrons); 1st and 4th Squadrons of the Hussars.

2nd Coy., 1st Artillery Bn.; 4th Coy., 2nd Artillery Bn.; 4th Coy., 3rd Artillery Bn.; 2nd Coy., 4th Artillery Bn.,; 1st Horse Artillery Company.

7 August 1805—Expedition to Germany under General Marmont:

Batavian Division Lt.-Gen. J. B. Dumonceau

1st Brigade Maj.-Gen. H. von Heldring; *2nd Brigade* Maj. Gen. H. F. A. von Hadel.

1st and 2nd Bns., 1st, 2nd, 6th and 8th Infantry Regiments; 1st Bn., 1st Light Infantry Regiment; 2nd Bn., 2nd Light Infantry Regiment; 2nd Bns. of the 1st and 2nd Regiment of Waldeck.

1st Dragoons (two squadrons); two squadrons of hussars.

2nd Coy., 1st Artillery Bn.; 4th and 5th Coys., 2nd Artillery Bn.; 1st and 4th Coys., 3rd Artillery Bn.; 1st Horse Artillery Coy.

Pontoneer detachment.

8 December 1805—Army of the North under Prince Louis Bonaparte:

Batavian Division Lt.-Gen. H. D. Bonhomme

1st Brigade Maj.-Gen. G. du Rij

1st and 2nd Bns., 4th Infantry Regiment; 1st and 2nd Bns., 7th Infantry Regiment; 2nd Bn., 1st Light Infantry Regiment.

1st Division of Foot Artillery.

Reserve Division of Foot Artillery.

2nd Brigade Col. Mascheck

1st and 2nd Bns. of the 3rd and 5th Infantry Regiments; 1st Bn., 2nd Light Infantry Regiment.

2nd Dragoons.

1st Division, Horse Artillery.

Uniforms, Kingdom of Holland, 1806-10

Grenadiers of the Guard

This regiment (the old Grenadiers of the Guard of the Council) was numbered '1' in the system of the Line Infantry; its uniform was very similar in style to that of the Grenadiers of the Imperial Guard but the colours were as follows: black bearskin bonnet with red plume and top patch with white grenade badge, white cords; white, long-tailed coat with crimson collar, cuffs, lapels and turnbacks, yellow buttons and yellow (gold for officers) lace loops with tassels at the outer ends to collar (two per side), cuffs (two) and lapels (seven). They wore red fringed epaulettes and had red sabre straps. Waistcoats, breeches and belts were white; the long gaiters were black.

Jagers of the Guard

This battalion was raised from the above-mentioned Grenadiers in 1806 and bore the number '1' in the series of Jager Battalions. It wore uniform as for the Grenadiers of the Guard but with green and yellow plumes and green fringed epaulettes with yellow crescents.

In 1810 the Guards infantry became the 2nd (later 3rd) Grenadiers of the Imperial Guard and retained their existing uniforms, only removing the yellow lace and adopting the Guards' button with the Imperial eagle.

The Line Infantry

Grenadiers wore black bearskin bonnets with red plumes, cords and top patch with white grenade badge; short-skirted white tunics, white waist-

13

'Dutch Jagers of various regiments of the VIII Army Corps in Hamburg'—Suhr's mention of the Corps dates this plate to the 1806–07 campaign against Prussia, Saxony and Russia when the 2nd and 3rd Jagers were in the 3rd Division. There seems to be total confusion here: we see three types of headgear, and although all have dark green coats and trousers, the 2nd Regt. is shown with both red and yellow facings, and the 3rd with both red and purple, or pink. All buttons are brass, all cords dark green, all shako numbers white and loops brass, all belts black. *Left to right (standing):* Carabinier, 3rd Regt.—red facings and epaulettes. Private, 2nd Regt., in waistcoat.

Carabinier, 2nd Regt.—red plume, cords and tassels on hat, facings, and epaulettes. Private, 3rd Regt.—yellow facings, dark green plume and epaulettes. *Left to right (seated):* Private, unit unknown, apparently wearing uniform of old 1st Jagers but has no shako number; plume yellow over dark green, no epaulettes, dark green facings piped red. Private, 2nd Regt.—dark green plume and epaulettes, red facings. Private, 3rd Regt.—dark green epaulettes, pink (?) piping to dark green facings. Private, 3rd Regt. (rear view)—dark green plume and epaulettes, yellow facings and piping.

coat, breeches and belts, short black gaiters; red epaulettes and sabre straps.

Fusiliers were dressed as above except that they had a shako with a large regimental number on the front; to the left side was a large brass loop, a button, and on top of the loop a pompon in the facing colour; white cords were worn. They had no epaulettes, but white shoulder-straps edged in the facing colour; and they carried no sabres.

Voltigeurs wore the shako with green cords and pompon, green epaulettes with yellow crescents, and green sabre straps; otherwise as for grenadiers. Officers wore gold gorgets, but no waist sashes. Their coat-tails were long, and they wore short boots.

The individual regimental facings were: 2nd—light blue, 3rd—red, 4th—pink, 5th—dark green, 6th—grass-green, 7th—yellow, 8th—light violet, and 9th—black. All buttons were brass.

In 1810 the infantry became the 123e–126e Ligne and the Walcheren Regiment (131e Ligne in 1811).

Jagers

The 1st and 2nd Light Infantry Regiments were retitled 1st and 2nd Jagers in 1806, then re-numbered 2nd and 3rd in the same year. Shakos as for the Line Infantry, dark green coats, lapels, shoulder-straps, waistcoats, breeches, pompons and cords. All buttons were brass. The 2nd Battalion had light blue facings, the 3rd yellow.

In 1810 the Jagers became the 33e Léger and wore French uniforms.

Guards Cavalry

The old Dragoons of the Guard were retitled 'Grenadiers te paard' in September 1806, and on 1 March 1807 were renamed and renumbered '1st Kurassiers of the Guard'. Their uniform was as for the Grenadiers of the Guard but with brass shoulder-scales instead of red epaulettes, and high-cuffed boots in place of the gaiters worn by their infantry comrades.

A regiment of Hussars of the Guard had been raised in 1805; it wore a black fur colpack, red dolman and breeches, yellow buttons and lace; white pelisse with black fur trim; blue and white sash, and white belts. In November 1807 it was retitled '1st Hussars'.

Line Cavalry

The 2nd Light Dragoons was converted to the '2nd Kurassiers' and wore the French-style brass cuirassier helmet with black crest and red plume, and a white coat with light blue facings, white buttons and red epaulettes. Belts were buff, waistcoat and breeches white. Apparently no cuirasses were worn.

The 2nd and 3rd Hussars wore the shako with the brass regimental number on the front, and above it a black cockade, brass loop and button, and black plume; white cords for parades. The 2nd Regiment wore dark blue dolman and breeches, the 3rd light blue; both wore yellow buttons and lace and had white belts, red and white sashes, and white dolmans with black fur trim. They carried brass-hilted sabres in brass-fitted black sheaths, and the plain black sabre-taches bore the regimental number in brass. It seems they wore white gauntlets. Their boots had yellow trim and tassel.

In 1810 the Guards cavalry became the 2nd (or Red) Lancers of the Imperial Guard; the 2nd Kurassiers became the 14e Cuirassiers; and the 2nd and 3rd Hussars became the 11e Hussards. They all wore French uniforms, as listed in the appropriate books in this series: *Napoleon's Guard Cavalry, Napoleon's Cuirassiers and Carabiniers* and *Napoleon's Hussars*.

Foot Artillery 1806

The Guards battery wore infantry-style uniform. The shako had a brass crown over crossed gun barrels at the front centre; to the left side a brass button and loop under a red pompon; and red cords. Dark blue coat and breeches, dark blue lapels; red collar, cuffs, turnbacks and epaulettes; brass buttons, black gaiters. Collar, lapels and cuffs bore the Guards' yellow tasselled lace. This battery bore the number '1'.

The three Line batteries dressed as above but with the following exceptions: no Guards' lace, dark blue cuff flaps, and shako pompons in battery colours: 2nd Battery—white, 3rd—light blue, 4th—yellow. All belts were white.

In 1810 they were combined into the 9e Régiment of French foot artillery and their new French uniforms were in the same colour scheme, but the shako received either the brass eagle plate or the

Carabinier (Jager-Grenadier), Voltigeur officer and Carabinier officer, 3rd Regt., Hamburg 1805–07. All uniforms dark green, facings and buttons yellow. The Carabinier has red plume, epaulettes and sabre strap, and yellow bearskin cords and chinscales. The Voltigeur officer in the centre has a dark green plume; both officers have gold epaulettes; and the Carabinier officer has a red plume and gold cords and chinscales, and powdered and queued hair.

rhombic plate, a French cockade, red cords and plume.

Horse Artillery 1806
Hussar-style uniform consisting of a shako with red top band, cords and plume, brass badge loop and button as for the foot artillery; dark blue dolman, pelisse and breeches; red lacing, yellow buttons and black belts.

In 1810 they were converted to the 7e Régiment of French horse artillery, wearing the same uniform but with French shako and cockade.

Engineers
As for the foot artillery but with white buttons.

Orders of Battle, 1806-10

7 October 1806—Part of VIII Corps in Germany under Marshal Marmont:
Royal Dutch Army King Ludwig of Holland
Garde Maj.-Gen. J. A. Colleart
Regiment of Grenadiers (two bns.), 1st Jagers (from 7 November).
Garde Kurassiers (three squadrons).
Artillery battery.
Line Troops (in two divisions)
1st and 2nd Bns. of the 2nd, 3rd and 7th Infantry Regiments.
Two squadrons each of the 2nd and 3rd Hussars and of the 2nd Kurassiers.
1st Coy., 2nd Artillery Bn.; 5th Coy., 3rd Artillery Bn.
Pontoneer detachment.
   On 7 November the 3rd Division (Gen. J. B. Dumonceau) joined the army in the field:
1st Bn., 4th Infantry Regiment; 1st Bn., 8th Infantry Regiment; 1st Bns. of the 2nd and 3rd Jager Regiments.
2nd Horse Artillery Company.

7 April 1807—In Swedish Pomerania, Prussia and Poland as part of the VIII Corps of Marshal Mortier:
Royal Dutch Army Corps Gen. J. B. Dumonceau
Advanced Guard Maj. Gen. C. L. Crass
1st, 2nd and 3rd Bns., 3rd Jager Regiment.
1st Division Lt.-Gen. S. J. Bruce
1st Brigade Maj.-Gen. H. von Heldring
1st and 2nd Bns., 3rd Infantry Regiment; 2nd Bns., 4th and 8th Infantry Regiments.
2nd Brigade Maj.-Gen. J. C. Abbems
1st and 2nd Bns. of the 6th and of the 9th Infantry Regiments.
Reserve
3rd Hussars.
Two foot artillery batteries.
Pontoneer detachment.
2nd Division Lt.-Gen. P. G. Gratien
1st Brigade Maj.-Gen. J. C. van Hasselt

Colour of the Batavian Guards of the Raadpensionaris Schimmelpenninck, 1805. White ground, gold edge embroidery, black corner grenades with red, yellow and grey flames. The centre is very similar to the 1802 model. Gold pike tip and cords. (After documents provided courtesy of Dutch Army Historical Section)

1st and 2nd Bns., 2nd Infantry Regiment; 1st Bn., 4th Infantry Regiment; 1st and 2nd Bns., 7th Infantry Regiment; 1st Bn., 8th Infantry Regiment.
2nd Brigade Maj.-Gen. C. Mascheck
2nd Hussars, 2nd Kurassiers.
1st and 2nd Horse Artillery Companies.
Battle Participation
2nd Kurassiers and 2nd Horse Artillery fought at Friedland; 2nd and 3rd Hussars and two foot artillery batteries fought at Stralsund.

1808–10—In Spain with the VI Corps of Marshal Lefebvre and later I Corps (Victor):
Dutch Brigade Maj.-Gen. D. H. Chasse
1st Bn., 2nd Infantry and 2nd Bn., 4th Infantry Regiments.
3rd Hussars.
3rd Horse Artillery Company.
One company of miners.
Battle Participation
31 October 1808—Durango; 17 March 1809—Mesa de Ibor; 27 March 1809—Ciudad Real; 15 May to 13 June 1809—defence of Merida; 28 June 1809—Talavera; 11 August 1809—Almonacid; 15 October 1809—Daymiel; 9 November 1809—Dos Barrios; 19 November 1809—Ocaña.

26 April 1809—With the X Corps under King Jerome of Westfalia:
Dutch Auxiliary Corps Lt.-Gen. P. G. Gratien
1st Brigade Maj.-Gen. Anthing
6th and 7th Infantry Regiments.
2nd Brigade Maj.-Gen. van Hasselt
8th and 9th Infantry Regiment.
Cavalry
2nd Kurassiers.
Artillery
1st Coy., 2nd Foot Battalion.
1st and 2nd Horse Companies.
Battle Participation
24 May—8th Infantry stormed Dömitz; 31 May—6th and 9th Infantry, 2nd Kurassiers and two horse artillery batteries stormed Stralsund and destroyed von Schill's rebel Prussian force.

Changes of Title, 1795-1814

Infantry of the Guard
Grenadiers A battalion of grenadiers of the Consular Guard was raised on 11 June 1805; in 1805 it was expanded into a regiment and in 1810 it became the 2e (then 3e) Grenadiers de la Garde Imperiale.
Jagers Two companies of Light Infantry of the Consular Guard were raised on 11 June 1805; on 18 July 1806 this was expanded to the Light Infantry Regiment and on 17 September 1806 retitled Jager Regiment. On 7 October 1807 it became the 3rd Bn., Grenadiers of the Guard and was disbanded on 29 November 1808.
Pupilles de la Garde On 1 September 1810 the 'Royal Dutch Velites' (orphans or sons of serving soldiers, aged fifteen to sixteen years old) entered French service; Napoleon reviewed them at the Tuilleries and was so impressed with their drill and bearing that on 1 June 1811 he took their nine battalions into the Imperial Guard as the 'Pupilles'. In April 1814 they declared for the provisional government of the Netherlands and adopted the orange cockade.

The Line Infantry

Half-Brigades 1795	Bat-talions 1803	Regiments 1805	1806	French Regiments 1810–1814
1st Bn., 1st	1	1	2	123ᵉ
2nd Bn., 1st	2			
3rd Bn., 1st	3	2	3	124ᵉ
1st Bn., 2nd	4			
2nd Bn., 2nd	5	3	4	125ᵉ
3rd Bn., 2nd	6	1	2	123ᵉ
1st Bn., 3rd	7	3	4	125ᵉ
2nd Bn., 3rd	8	1	2	123ᵉ
3rd Bn., 3rd	9	7	8	disbanded
1st Bn., 4th	10	8	9	126ᵉ
2nd Bn., 4th	11	4	5	1807, 'Zeeuwsche Legion'; 1810, Regiment van Walcheren 1811, 131ᵉ.
3rd Bn., 4th	12			
1st Bn., 5th	13	6	7	disbanded
2nd Bn., 5th	14			
3rd Bn., 5th	15	5	6	disbanded
1st Bn., 6th	16			
2nd Bn., 6th	17	6	7	disbanded
3rd Bn., 6th	18			
1st Bn., 7th	19	8	9	126ᵉ
2nd Bn., 7th	20			
3rd Bn., 7th	21	7	8	disbanded

Jager and Light Infantry

Jagers 1795	Light Infantry Regiments 1805	Jager Regiments 1806	1807	1809	French Regiments 1810–14
1st Bn.	1st	1st then 2nd	Dis-banded 1 April		
2nd Bn.					
3rd Bn.	2nd	2nd then 3rd	2nd	1st	33ᵉ Léger
4th Bn.					

The Foreign Regiments

1795	Infantry Regiments 1806	
1st Waldeck	Part of 3rd Bn., 1st, then 3rd/2nd	
2nd Waldeck	Part of 3rd Bn., 2nd, then 3rd/3rd	Disbanded 1808
Sachsen-Gotha	Part of 3rd Bn., 6th, then 3rd/7th	

Dutch Colonial 'Guides of Surinam', 1815, after Teupken. Orange hat cockade, dark blue jacket with white piping and buttons, white and light blue checked neckcloth. The pack appears to be of raffia or split cane on a square frame.

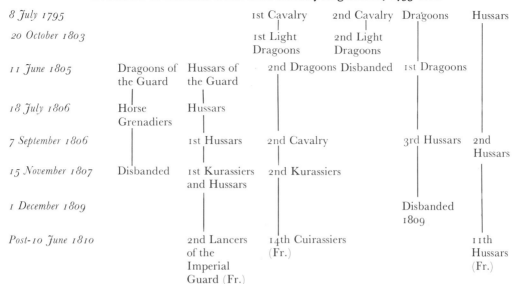

8 July 1795			1st Cavalry	2nd Cavalry	Dragoons	Hussars
20 October 1803			1st Light Dragoons	2nd Light Dragoons		
11 June 1805	Dragoons of the Guard	Hussars of the Guard	2nd Dragoons	Disbanded	1st Dragoons	
18 July 1806	Horse Grenadiers	Hussars				
7 September 1806		1st Hussars	2nd Cavalry		3rd Hussars	2nd Hussars
15 November 1807	Disbanded	1st Kurassiers and Hussars	2nd Kurassiers			
1 December 1809					Disbanded 1809	
Post-10 June 1810		2nd Lancers of the Imperial Guard (Fr.)	14th Cuirassiers (Fr.)			11th Hussars (Fr.)

The Uniforms of 1814-15

The Belgian Legion

When in 1814 the Belgian provinces fell under Austrian control, they raised a Belgian Legion which included infantry, cavalry and artillery. The infantry wore Austrian shakos with the brass initials 'LB' on the front; white Austrian infantry coats with regimental facings shown on collar, Polish cuffs, turnbacks and piping to shoulder-straps and front of jacket, and brass buttons; French badges of rank; white breeches and belts; short, black gaiters. The regimental facings were: 1st Regiment—green, 2nd—yellow, 3rd—light blue, and 4th—red. The Chevau-Légers of the Legion wore black Austrian cavalry helmets with a white metal front plate bearing 'LB' in brass, white metal combe and fittings, and yellow 'sausage' crest; dark green, single-breasted tunics with lemon-yellow collar, Polish cuffs, turnbacks and front piping; white belts and buttons; dark green breeches, and plain hussar boots.

Later in 1814 the Belgian Legion was absorbed into the newly formed Dutch-Belgian army; the infantry became separate battalions in the Line (which are not known) and the cavalry became the 5th Light Dragoons.

The Regiment of Nassau-Oranien

A foreign unit, the Regiment Nassau-Oranien

Dragoons in stable dress, 1805–07. All uniforms dark blue, the fatigue caps with white piping and badges and red tassels. Red facings and white buttons. The man on the left has white epaulette fringes and white turnback grenades, and the two right-hand figures seem to wear short waistcoats with full regimental facings.

19

passed into the service of the new Kingdom of the Netherlands on 8 November 1814 and allocated the number '28' in 1815. It wore the Nassau army uniform of shako (but with crowned 'W' in brass on the front) with orange cockade; dark green coat, with black collar and cuffs and yellow buttons and piping; dark green trousers; white belts, and black gaiters.

The Dutch-Belgian Army, 1814–15

In 1814 the Line infantry was rapidly organized into sixteen battalions dressed as follows: Austrian infantry shako with front and rear peaks, crowned brass shield bearing the cypher 'W', orange cockade, white loop, yellow button and white plume. Dark blue, single-breasted tunic of British pattern with dark blue shoulder-straps and cuff

Dutch Infantry Colours, 1806–10. Gold pike tip and nails; gold inscriptions; white ground; red and blue corners; the lion in natural colours. Colours of this pattern were presented to all infantry regiments—Guards, Line and Jagers—in February/March 1807. That of the 2nd Bn., 5th Infantry illustrated here was captured by the British at Veere in Zealand in 1809, and a copy of it hangs in the Royal Hospital, Chelsea (the original has, alas, fallen apart). In 1811 the 'new' French regiments received 1804 pattern colours with their eagles from the Emperor, and in May 1812 these were changed for 1811 tricolour models. (After documents provided courtesy of Dutch Army Historical Section)

flaps piped in the facing colour, which was worn also on collar, cuffs and tunic front piping. Turn-backs were red, buttons yellow, belts white, trousers grey and gaiters black. Flank companies (grenadiers and light companies) were distinguished by dark blue shoulder-rolls piped white; grenadiers had white plumes tipped with red, and light companies white tipped with green. Facings were as follows: 1st* and 9th Battalions—orange, 2nd* and 10th†—yellow; 3rd and 11th†—white; 4th* and 12th—red; 5th† and 13th—crimson; 6th and 14th—light green; 7th and 15th—light blue; 8th and 16th—pink.

In January 1815 regimental facings were discontinued, and all line units henceforth wore white. The 16th Battalion was a Jager unit and wore a green coat faced yellow; their karabinier company had green plumes tipped with red, the light company green tipped with yellow, the centre companies plain green. They had black belts. Belgian units wore the famous 'Belgic cap' adopted by the British infantry in 1812; the plume or tuft was worn at the left side of this, and white

Unmarked units are Dutch metropolitan
*Belgian
†Dutch colonial

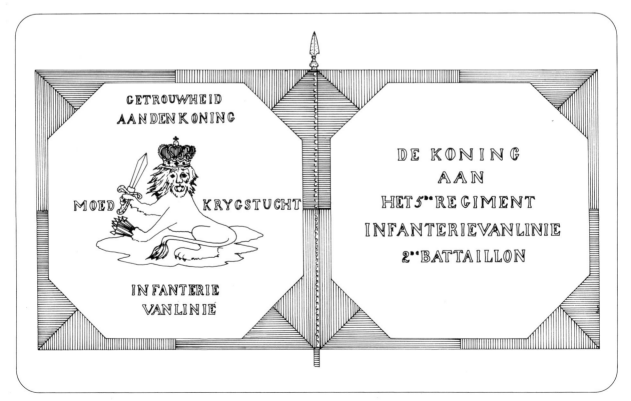

2nd Kurassiers in Hamburg, November 1807. The left man wears the old 1st Light Dragon uniform with red turban and black facings, while the right man wears the new uniform with helmet of French cuirassier design; light blue facings; white buttons; red plume, epaulettes and service stripes. Leatherwork for both is buff, and scabbards brass.

units wore a brass stringed bugle under the battalion number on their shakos. Rank badges were very similar to the French system:

General—Two gold bullion epaulettes with four six-pointed silver stars, and gold or silver sabre strap in the button colour. *Lieutenant-General*—As above but with three stars. *Major-General*—With two stars. *Colonel*—Two epaulettes in the button colour with bullion fringes. *Lieutenant-Colonel*—As above but with contrasting lace down the straps (i.e. gold on silver and vice versa). *Major*—As for Lieutenant-Colonel but two contrasting stripes. *Captain*—One bullion fringed epaulette in the button colour, on the right. *Lieutenant*—As for captain but with light fringes. *Adjutants*—One such epaulette, left. *Sous-Adjutant*—Two fringeless epaulettes in the button colour. *Sergeant-major*—Two chevrons, point up, in the button colour (gold or silver) above the cuff, and a silver sabre strap with orange tassel. *Sergeant*—One such chevron, and the sabre strap. *Corporal*—Two woollen chevrons in the button colour, and white strap with orange tassel. *Lance-Corporal*—One chevron in the facing colour.

Later in 1815 (probably after the battle of Waterloo) a new model shako was issued. It had no neck shield; above the peak was a pointed brass plate extending to the chin-strap bosses and bearing the battalion/regimental number; above this was the orange cockade, and the loop and button.

The following single-battalion units were raised in 1815: 17th and 18th Dutch Jagers; 19th–26th Dutch colonial infantry; 27th Dutch Jagers; 28th (Regiment Nassau-Oranien); 33rd Dutch colonial depot battalion; 34th (Garrison); 35th* Jagers; 36th* Jagers. All Jager units wore the uniform of the 16th Jagers. More foreign troops were also taken into Dutch service in the form of four Swiss regiments each of two battalions: 29th (Berne); 30th (Zürich); 31st (Grisson); 32nd (Roman Cantons). These Swiss regiments had the new shako (post-Waterloo); dark blue, single-breasted tunics with nine bars of regimental lace across the chest and regimental facings on collar, cuffs and turnbacks, as follows: 29th *a* (facings)—red, *b* (buttons, lace and flank company wings)—white; 30th *a*—orange, *b*—white; 31st *a*—light blue, *b*—white; 32nd *a*—yellow, *b*—yellow.

cords decorated the front under the brass plate bearing a 'W'. Musicians were distinguished by wings in the facing colour, edged yellow. Jager

The 2nd Kurassiers in Hamburg, 1808—all wear yellow buttons, for some reason unexplained. *Left to right:* Trooper, foul weather dress, in black oilskin helmet cover, grey cape and overalls. Trumpeter, undress, with white helmet crest and red plume; light blue surtout with yellow facings and piping; buff waistcoat; grey overalls with black leather vandyking; brass trumpet, light blue and white mixed cords; brass scabbard. Trumpeter, parade dress, with black crest, red plume; light blue tunic, white collar and lapels edged gold; white lace and epaulettes; trumpet as before. Trooper, parade dress and cloak; black crest, red plume; white tunic, waistcoat and breeches, with light blue facings; grey caped cloak.

There were also 45 battalions of militia infantry (1st–20th Dutch, 21st–45th Belgian); they wore English 'stovepipe' shakos with white metal sunburst plate, orange cockade, white button and loop and white plume; dark blue coat as for the line infantry with orange facings on collar, plain round cuffs, piping on coat front and around dark blue shoulder-straps; white turnbacks and buttons; grey trousers over short, black gaiters; white belts.

Infantry drummers had white 'swallow's nests' laced and trimmed in yellow braid and with white and yellow mixed fringes, and a brass drum with hoops painted in triangles in sequence white-red-blue.

Cavalry

In 1814 two regiments of heavy dragoons were raised and were given a very old-fashioned uniform consisting of a large bicorn with orange cockade, and white plume, loop, button and tassels; dark blue, long-tailed tunic with facings shown on collar, lapels, cuffs and turnbacks (pink for the 1st Regiment and yellow for the 2nd); white buttons, belts and waistcoat; buff breeches; high-cuffed boots; heavy cavalry sword with brass hilt in steel sheath; white gauntlets. By 1815 there were eight line cavalry regiments dressed as follows:

1st (Dutch) Karabiniers The 1st Heavy Dragoons of 1814. Steel helmet with brass combe, chinscales, edging and lion's head on the front; black 'sausage' crest; white plume on left side. Dark blue, short-tailed, single-breasted coat with pink facings on collar and cuffs and pink piping; dark blue shoulder-straps piped pink; white belts, buttons, gauntlets and breeches; red turnbacks with yellow grenades. Dark blue, square shabraque and portmanteau bordered white, outer piping red; white sheepskin (black for officers) edged with vandyking in the facing colour; black harness with white fittings. Trumpeters had a white crest; red plume and tunic; red collar; dark blue lapels, cuffs and turnbacks; brass trumpet, white cords mixed with red.

2nd (Belgian) Karabiniers As above except double-breasted tunic with dark blue collar piped red; red lapels, cuffs, turnbacks and epaulettes (white for trumpeters). White grenade badges to saddle furniture. Grenade badge to brass belt-plate; brass-hilted sword in steel sheath.

3rd (Dutch) Karabiniers The old 2nd Heavy Dragoons of 1814. As for 1st Regiment but with yellow facings.

4th (Dutch) Light Dragoons Black French-style shako with crowned white metal plate bearing a 'W'; brass chinscales; white top band and cords; white cockade loop and button, and black plume. Dark blue, short-tailed, single-breasted tunic; red collar, pointed cuffs, turnbacks (with white hunting horn badges); white buttons and lace trim to collar, cuffs, shoulder-straps, chest (in hussar fashion) and rear of jacket. Plain black leather sabretache and pouch; white belts; grey overalls with black booting and white side stripe. Dark blue pointed shabraque and round port-

Sapeur and private, 3rd Regt.; Voltigeur, 2nd, and Musketier, 4th Regts., all in the post-1806 uniform. *Left to right:* Fusilier private, 3rd Regt., with red plume; white cords, loop, button and '3'; red facings. Sapeur in undress, with red plume, facings, epaulettes, piping, arm badge, and sabre strap, and white grenades on turnbacks. Musician of Musketiers, 4th Regt., with white decorative band at top of shako, white cords and '4'; white buttons; pink collar, cuffs, lapels and turnbacks. Voltigeur of '2nd Regt.'—either the shako number or the facings seem wrong, as written sources list light blue facings from 1806, and this figure wears red. Fusilier, 3rd Regt. in barrack dress; white and red cap, white waistcoat with red collar and white buttons.

manteau edged white; white sheepskin edged red. Trumpeters wore red plumes and tunics.

5th (Belgian) Light Dragoons (Ex-Chevau-Légers of the Belgian Legion of 1814.) As for 4th except: green shako, black plume with yellow tip; dark green, double-breasted tunic; lemon yellow collar, lapels, pointed cuffs, turnbacks and piping; white buttons; green trouser stripe. Officers had green plumes. Dark green saddle furniture edged yellow. This was their original uniform of 1814. Trumpeters wore red plumes and yellow coats faced green.

6th (Dutch) Hussars Black, French-style shako; brass crowned 'W' badge; yellow top band; yellow and black cords; white loop and button; orange cockade; brass chinscales. Light blue dolman and breeches; dark blue pelisse, black fur; yellow and black lace; yellow buttons; white and orange barrel sash; white belts; black sabre-tache with brass crowned 'W'. Red shabraque edged in yellow-black-yellow lace; yellow crowned 'W' badge; light blue portmanteau edged yellow; yellow edging to sheepskin. Trumpeters wore red plumes, dolman and breeches, and light blue pelisse, otherwise as above.

7th (Colonial) Hussars (In the East Indies in 1815.) Tall, red stovepipe shako with white cords and plume; light blue dolman and breeches; red collar and cuffs; white lace and buttons; orange sash; white belts. Trumpeters wore red plumes, dolmans and breeches.

8th (Belgian) Hussars (The old Hussards de Croy.) Tall, black stovepipe shako with white metal crowned cypher 'W'; white top band, loop and button; orange cockade; black plume; light blue dolman, pelisse and breeches; red collar and cuffs; white buttons and lace; black fur; red and white sash. Black sabretache with white crowned 'W' for the men. Officers had white shako plumes, white fur trim to pelisses, silver lace and buttons, and red sabretaches edged white and with a white crowned 'W' badge. Trumpeters wore red shako, dolman and pelisse, light blue collar and cuffs.

Foot Artillery Austrian-pattern shako with brass-crowned front plate, yellow cockade loop and button, and black plume with red tip. Dark blue infantry-style coat with red turnbacks; red piping to black collar and cuffs, dark blue cuff flaps and shoulder-straps and to front and bottom edges of coat; brass buttons; white belts; grey trousers.

Horse Artillery As above but plain black plume; shako badge has a crown over crossed cannon barrels; turnback badges of black grenades; red shoulder wings piped yellow; dark blue shabraque and round portmanteau edged red with red crowned 'W' badge; red edging to white sheepskin. Trumpeters wore red with black facings.

Engineers As for Foot Artillery but light blue collar and round cuffs; red turnbacks and piping to coat front; dark blue wings trimmed light blue.

Train Horse artillery shako with white metal badge; grey, single-breasted coat and shoulder-straps; black collar, cuffs and cuff flaps all piped red; red piping to jacket front; red turnbacks; white buttons; grey overalls with red side stripe; black belts.

The 1815 Campaign

Royal Netherlands Army in June 1815

Mobile Army H.R.H. William Prince of Orange

Corps under command of II British Corps (Lord Hill) H.R.H. Frederik, Prince of the Netherlands

Indian Brigade (strength 3,583: Lt.-Gen. C. H. W. Anthing

5th Regiment, East India Infantry (2 bns.); 10th and 11th Bns., West Indian Rifles (Jagers); 1st Flank Bn. (European companies of the 19th, 20th, 21st, 22nd, 23rd and 24th Bns., East India Infantry); one battery of foot artillery (8 guns).

1st Division (divisional strength 6,389 men): Lt.-Gen. J. A. Stedman

1st Brigade Maj.-Gen. B. d'Hauw

16th Jagers; 4th and 6th Line and 9th, 14th and 15th Militia Bns.

2nd Brigade Maj.-Gen. D. J. de Berens

18th Jagers; 1st Line and 1st, 2nd and 18th Militia Bns.

One foot artillery battery (Capt. P. Wynands)— 8 guns.

2nd Division Lt.-Gen. H. G. Baron de Perponcher. (This division fought at Quatre Bras and Waterloo.)

1. Jager, 4th Jager Battalion, 1801
2. Grenadier, Infantry Regiment Waldeck, 1801
3. Jager of Light Infantry, 1801

A

Trooper, 2nd Cavalry Regiment, 1801

B

1. Officer, 22nd Infantry Battalion, 1803
2. Officer, 1st Cavalry Regiment, 1804
3. Trooper, 1st Light Dragoons, 1804

C

1. Fusilier Private, Line Infantry, 1801
2. Karabinier of Light Infantry, 1801
3. Private, Centre Companies, 1st Regiment, Dutch Brigade, 1799—1802

D

1. Gunner, Horse Artillery, Kingdom of Holland, 1806—10
2. Gunner, Artillery of the Royal Guard, 1806-10
3. Corporal, Dragoons of the Line, 1805

E

1. Officer, Jagers of the Guard, 1806—10
2. Trooper, Chevau-Légers, Belgian Legion, 1814
3. Corporal of Flanquers, Belgian Infantry, 1815

F

1. Trooper, 6th Dutch Hussars, 1815
2. Officer, 5th (Belgian) Light Dragoons, 1815
3. Trumpeter, 2nd (Belgian) Karabiniers, 1815

G

1. Lieutenant, Dutch Infantry, 1815
2. Hornist of Flanquers, 16th (Dutch) Jagers, 1815
3. National Militiaman 1st Class

H

1st Brigade Maj.-Gen. W. F. Count de Bylandt 27th Jagers (strength 809); 7th Line (701) and 5th (482), 7th (675) and 8th (566) Militia Bns. One horse artillery battery (Capt. A. Bijleveld) — 8 guns.

2nd Brigade Col. F. W. Goedecke
2nd Regiment of Nassau (three bns.) (2,709); 28th Regiment 'Nassau-Oranien' (two bns.) (1,427); volunteer Jager coy. (169).
One foot artillery battery (Capt. E. J. Stevenart) — 8 guns.

3rd Division Lt.-Gen. D. H. Baron Chassé. (At Braine l'Alleud at start of Waterloo.)

1st Brigade Col. H. Detmers
35th Jagers (605); 2nd Line (471); 4th (519), 6th (492), 17th (534) and 19th (467) Militia Bns. One horse artillery battery (Capt. C. F. Krahmer de Bichin) — 8 guns.

2nd Brigade Maj.-Gen. Count d'Aubremé
36th Jagers (633); 3rd Line (629); 3rd (592), 10th (632), 12th (431) and 13th (664) Militia Bns. One foot artillery battery (Capt. J. H. Lux) — 8 guns.

Cavalry Division Lt.-Gen. J. A. Baron de Collaert

Heavy Brigade Maj.-Gen. Jonkheer A. D. Trip
1st (446), 2nd (399) and 3rd (392) Karabiniers.
1st Light Brigade Maj.-Gen. C. E. Baron de Ghignij
4th Light Dragoons (647); 8th Hussars (439).
2nd Light Brigade Maj.-Gen. J. B. Baron van Merlen
5th Light Dragoons (441); 6th Hussars (641).
Two half-batteries of horse artillery (Captains A. Petter and A. R. W. Geij van Pittius) each of 4 guns.

In the fortresses were: 8th, 9th, 14th and 15th Line Bns., 17th Jagers, and the 11th, 12th, 13th, 16th and 20th Militia. In training were the 21st–47th Militia Bns., the 29th–32nd Swiss Infantry Regiments, the 33rd Depot Bn. and the 34th Garrison Bn. In the East Indies were the 7th Hussars and the 19th–26th Bns. of East Indian Infantry.

★   ★   ★

There is limited space in this book to devote to the details of the battles of Quatre Bras and Waterloo in which the Netherlands troops took part; detailed accounts of Quatre Bras are contained in my books *The Black Brunswickers* and *Napoleon's German Allies (2): Nassau and Oldenburg*, and further details of both battles are contained in these books and in *The King's German Legion*, also in this series.

The Netherlands troops which fought at Quatre Bras on 16 June were: the 2nd Brigade (Colonel Goedecke) of Perponcher's 2nd Division — who were the first Allied troops on the field; the 1st Brigade (Major-General Count de Bylandt) of the 2nd Division — who reinforced their comrades during the morning; and the 2nd Light Cavalry Brigade of General van Merlen. The fighting that day against Ney's troops was hard and bloody, and although the Allies threw back all French thrusts, Wellington ordered a withdrawal northwards that night (16 June) because the Prussian defeat at the hands of the French at Ligny on the same day exposed his left flank and made the Quatre Bras position liable to be outflanked. The Allied army was ordered to concentrate near Waterloo to block Napoleon's inevitable thrust on Brussels. The map of the battle gives the dispositions of the Netherlands troops. Losses were about 4,000 dead and wounded on each side at Quatre Bras, and van Merlen's cavalry brigade had suffered a reverse at the hands of Piré's cavalry during the day. One Netherlands artillery captain made a 'cavalry' charge with the crews of his half-battery during the desperate fighting to drive off Piré's light cavalry, which had captured a battery of foot artillery and were attempting to take off the guns.

The Battle of Waterloo
Dispositions of the Netherlands forces on this fateful field are shown on the accompanying map, and it will be seen that Bylandt's 1st Brigade of the 2nd Division was placed in an exposed position, on a forward slope in the Allied centre, directly where any French assault would be bound to fall. This brigade had already fought at Quatre Bras and had withdrawn to its present position; thus its morale can scarcely have been soaring, particularly when faced with the entire might of the French army.

The following data, kindly provided by the Chief of the Historical Section, Royal Netherlands Army, throws some vital light onto the

Beating the Retreat by musicians of various regiments in Hamburg, 1807–08. *Left to right:*

Drummer, 3rd Regt., old uniform—white plume and cords, dark blue coat faced red, white buttons and lace, brass drum with red and white hoops.

Grenadier drummer, 7th Regt., old uniform—red plume and epaulettes, yellow facings, white buttons and lace, red and light blue drum hoops.

Fusilier drummer, 3rd Regt., new uniform—as for first figure except white coat, white '3', and red, white and blue drum hoops.

Grenadier drummer, 6th Regt., new uniform—red plume and epaulettes, light green facings, white buttons, white cords and brass plate on cap, light blue drum hoops.

Voltigeur fifer, 2nd Regt., new uniform (obscured)—dark green plume, pink (should be light blue) facings.

Voltigeur fifer, 9th Regt., new uniform—dark green epaulettes; dark green pompon, black cockade and white loop, all centrally placed; black facings edged with black and white dicing.

Fusilier drummer, 4th Regt., new uniform—white pompon apparently with pink '4', pink facings, light blue and white drum hoops.

controversy which often surrounds the participation of the Dutch-Belgian army at Quatre Bras and Waterloo. It may be new to many readers, and should certainly stimulate interest in further research into this subject. The hitherto unquestioned validity of accepted British sources on this topic may now be viewed in a new, and more critical, light.

'As for your third question, the background was too complicated to answer in a short way,

Map of Quatre Bras, 16 June 1815, showing the relative positions of the 2nd Regt. of Nassau, the Regt. Nassau-Oranien, and four of the infantry battalions of Gen. Bylandt's Dutch-Belgian brigade and the sixteen divisional guns. 1 = Gemioncourt farm; 2 = Lairal farm; 3 = Grand Pierrepoint farm; 4 = Petit Pierrepoint farm; 5 = Marais; 6 = Frasnes les Rous.

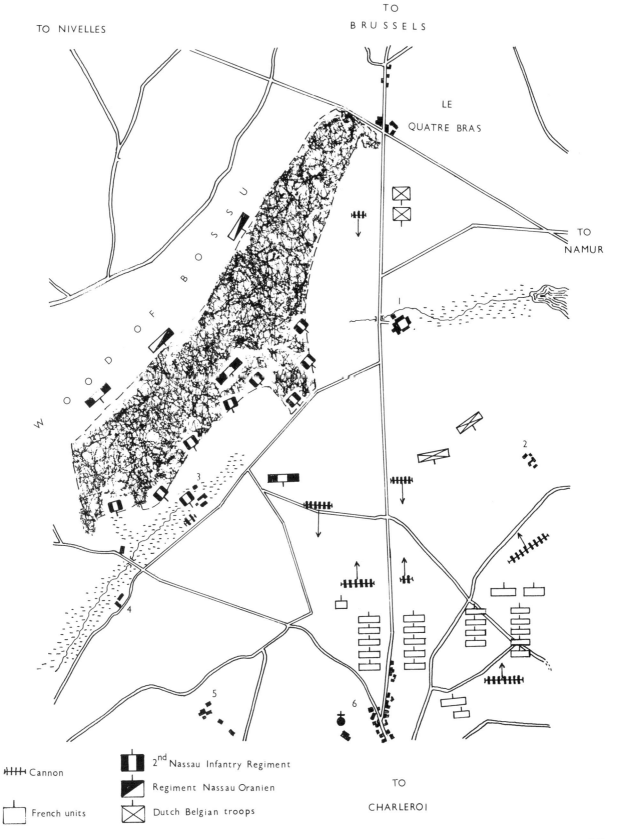

TO NIVELLES

TO
BRUSSELS

LE
QUATRE BRAS

TO
NAMUR

W
O
O
D
OF
BOSSU

TO

CHARLEROI

HIHI Cannon

2nd Nassau Infantry Regiment

Regiment Nassau Oranien

Dutch Belgian troops

French units

27

because there are many misunderstandings on this subject as a result of the rather misleading book of Captain W. Siborne (*History of the War in France and Belgium in 1815*).

'As we have observed through the years, that book is unfortunately repeated by military historians up to this very day.

'The following account is based on the official report of General de Perponcher of 11 July 1815, and the historical account of the Second Division by the chief of staff of that division, Colonel van Zuylen van Nyevelt, on 25 October 1815 (papers which were never seen or asked for by Captain Siborne).

'As you know, Bylandt's brigade had suffered heavy losses at Quatre Bras and received orders to move north. On 17 June at about 18.00 it received orders from the General Headquarters of Wellington to take up positions on the (exposed) forward slope, south of the "hollow road" to Ohain near Mont Saint Jean.

'The brigade was charged with outpost duties, and, as a covering force, was unable to rest. As a result of a false alarm it manned battle positions at about 02.00 on 18 June. In the morning of 18 June, on special request of the Prince of Orange, there was a (very limited) resupply of ammunition. The brigade was practically without ammunition since Quatre Bras. Simultaneously some meagre soup was given to the troops. The brigade came that day under the orders of General Picton.

'N.B. In view of the following statements it will always be a mystery, who ordered the brigade in that position and gave it that strange mission. General Gomm* [then Chief of Staff of Picton's division]: "I did not place them in that dangerous position." Sir James Shaw Kennedy† (of Wellington's staff): "It was a highly irresponsible deployment of troops."

'During his inspection in that sector on 18 June between 10.00 and 11.00, Wellington did not change the strange and impossible position of the Netherlands brigade.

'At about 11.00 enemy attack preparations and concentrations of artillery were observed by the brigade. Whereupon General de Perponcher ordered the brigade to move north of the "hollow road" to form one line with Picton's division. He made an end to a very dangerous situation, and the brigade filled the gap between Kempt's brigade (right) and Pack's brigade (left). At about 12.00 Bylandt's brigade was in position with two firing lines.

'At about 13.00 the impressive cannonade started, which continued until about 14.00, when the bombardment lifted for a few moments while d'Erlon's army corps marched through the intervals of the guns and started down the slope. General Picton ordered Kempt and Pack to form battalion squares. The column Donzelot, reinforced with Bourgeois's brigade (total 7,000 men) charged across the "hollow road" on Bylandt's brigade, which was then still in line formation, with the 5th Battalion in reserve (second line). Forced by the massive attack the first line moved back over a distance of 100 yards to the back of the second line, and together formed a square.

'N.B. This normal combat procedure was explained by Siborne as a flight. Furthermore he let the so-called "flight" start at the forward slope, which by a tactical decision was already left by the brigade at about 11.30!

'Under the command of Colonel van Zuylen van Nyevelt, the battalions of Bylandt's brigade then joined in the counter-attack of Kempt's and Pack's brigades.‡ During this attack, by which the French were forced to retreat south of the "hollow road", two horses were killed under General de Perponcher. General van Bylandt, Colonel van Zuylen van Nyevelt and three battalion commanders were wounded.

'General van Bylandt, being wounded, gave the command of the brigade to the last battalion commander, Lieutenant-Colonel de Jongh, who, already wounded at Quatre Bras, managed to control the battle by letting himself be roped to the saddle.

'I hope that this account has cleared up the fate of Bylandt's brigade and that the information may tend to the value of your book.'

*In a letter to Captain Siborne

† *The Campaign of Waterloo — A Military History* by John Codman Ropes (US).

‡See the statements of Major-General Kempt and Captain Mounsteven of the 28th Regiment of Foot.

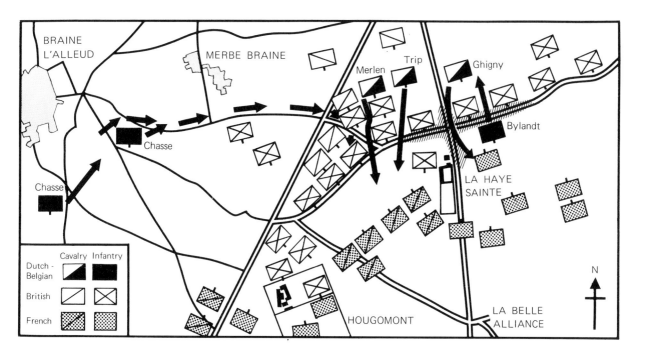

The three Dutch-Belgian cavalry brigades were initially deployed as part of the Allied reserve behind the centre; at about 14.00hrs they were sent against advancing French cavalry. The Heavy Brigade clashed with 7e and 12e Cuirassiers between Hougomont and La Haye Sainte; the 1st Light Brigade fought with the 3e and 4e Lanciers between La Haye Sainte and Papelotte, then moved to the Allied right flank and charged the Grenadiers à Cheval of the Imperial Guard during the series of massed French cavalry assaults at this point. After this clash they were so cut up that they were ordered back to regroup in the rear. The 2nd Light Brigade advanced to help throw back the French infantry assault east of La Haye Saint, and was then transferred to the west flank, where it supported Maitland's guards in their decisive action against the Imperial Guard. They had a hard action here against the Chasseurs à Cheval and the Lanciers of the Imperial Guard. They then moved east and clashed with the 1e Cuirassiers during the massed cavalry assaults before being pulled back to regroup. All three cavalry brigades took part in the general pursuit that night.

From a starting strength of 3,405 men and slightly more horses, Collaert's division lost 937 men and 945 horses killed and wounded this day. Collaert and van Merlen were killed, and the four regimental commanders were wounded.

Map showing positions of Dutch-Belgian formations at Waterloo on 18 June 1815. Bylandt's exposed infantry brigade is shown in its original position, with its move to the rear at about 11.30am indicated. The three cavalry brigades are shown with the directions of their first charges against the advancing French. Those infantry units initially deployed at Braine l'Alleud did not come up to the battlefield in time to take part in the main fighting of the day, although Chasse's infantry did take part in the final repulse of the Middle Guard. Goedecke's brigade, the 2nd Nassau and Nassau-Oranien regiments, were above Papelotte and Smohain, slightly off the eastern edge of this map. See also the Men-at-Arms title *Napoleon's German Allies (2): Nassau and Oldenburg*.

Losses of the 2nd Division and the 2nd Light Cavalry Brigade at Quatre Bras 15 and 16 June 1815

Units	Strength	Total casualties	As a percentage
2nd Division:			
27th Jagers	809	263	32.5
7th Line	701	94	13.4
5th Militia	482	303	62.9
7th Militia*	675	nil	—
8th Militia	566	25	4.4
2nd Regt. Nassau	2,709	143†	5.3
28th Regt. 'Nassau-Oranien'	1,581	nil	—
Volunteer Jager Company	177	17	9.6
Artillery	226	68‡	30.1
Train	251	nil	—
Total	8,177	913	11.2

*Arrived late

†35 lost on 15 June between Frasnes and Quatre Bras

‡5 lost on 15 June between Frasnes and Quatre Bras

Units	Strength	Total casualties	As a percentage
2nd Light Cavalry Brigade:			
5th Light Dragoons	441	171	38.8
6th Hussars	641	49	7.6
Total	1,082	220	20.3

Losses on 15, 16 and 18 June 1815

	Killed or missing		Wounded	
	Officers	Men	Officers	Men
2nd Division:				
H.Q.			2	
Staff	1		3	
27th Jager	1	170	5	172
7th Line	2	100	6	134
5th National Militia	3	172	7	132
7th National Militia	1	221	7	57
8th National Militia		87	7	103
1st Bn., 2nd Regt. of Nassau	1	85	5	92
2nd Bn., 2nd Regt. of Nassau	1	58	10	86
3rd Bn., 2nd Regt. of Nassau		21	8	105
1st Bn., Regt. 'Nassau-Oranien' No. 28	1	24	3	33
2nd Bn., Regt. 'Nassau-Oranien' No. 28		58	4	42
Artillery and Train	1	28	6	83
Total 2nd Division	12	1,024	73	1,039
3rd Division:				
Staff			1	
35th Jagers		8	3	60
2nd Line		55	4	34
4th National Militia		44		26
6th National Militia	1	26		15
17th National Militia		31	1	24
19th National Militia		51	1	25
36th Jägers		44		10
3rd Line		57	2	23
12th Line		10		13
13th Line		40		20
3rd National Militia		7		26
10th National Militia		10		24
Artillery and Train		27		21
Total 3rd Division	1	410	12	321
Cavalry Division				
Staff	1		2	
Regt. Karabiniers No. 1	2	25	9	66
Regt. Karabiniers No. 2	1	87	4	64
Regt. Karabiniers No. 3		32	2	29
Regt. Light Dragoons No. 4	4	101	8	135
Regt. Hussars No. 8	1	132	7	145
Regt. Light Dragoons No. 5		81	2	74
Regt. Hussars No. 6	3	141	6	64
Horse Artillery and Train		17	1	19
Total Cavalry Division	12	616	41	596
Grand Total	25	2,050	126	1,956

= 4,157 men and 1,630 horses

Colours and Standards

Batavian Republic 1795–1806:

Colours of the 1795 pattern were presented to the six Half-Brigades then in existence on 11 September 1795 at a scale of one per battalion, and on 14 March 1796 three more were presented to the 7th Half-Brigade. These colours were silk with the designs painted on them, and were relatively fragile; replacements were issued as follows:

25 January 1800—3rd Battalion/1st Half-Brigade

19 March 1800—1st/7th and 3rd/7th

25 April 1800—1st/3rd

17 October 1800—1st/2nd and 2nd/2nd

30 November 1801—2nd/4th

Colours of the 1802 pattern were presented as follows:

28 May 1802—22nd and 23rd Infantry Battalions

9 November 1802—3rd/5th

20 December 1802—1st and 2nd Regiments of Waldeck (with the crest of the Prince of Waldeck on the reverse)

4th June 1804—all other units had 1802 pattern colours ordered for them.

The new regiments formed in 1805 received no new colours; only the Grenadier Guards of the Council were presented with two colours shortly after formation. No data is available concerning cavalry standards in this period.

Band of the 7th Regiment in Hamburg. The drum-major has a yellow plume with white tip; yellow facings with silver lace at collar, cuffs and 'swallow's nests'; yellow and silver bandolier. The musicians all wear yellow coats with white (silver?) lace at collar and cuff, and yellow and white plumes. Note the negro with the 'Jingling Johnny'.

The Kingdom of Holland 1806–10:

New colours were presented to some units by King Ludwig at the Hague on 7 February 1807, and these were the red and blue quartered design with the white central octagon bearing the dedication and the lion. Cavalry standards were smaller but of similar design.

Colours and standards issued to Guards units were very similar to the French 1804 pattern; light blue with white central lozenge, in the centre of the obverse the royal crest instead of the lion carried by the Line.

On 22 March 1807, Marshal Count Dumonceau presented colours at Bremen to the following units, at a scale of one per battalion: 2nd and 3rd Jagers; 2nd, 3rd and 7th Line Infantry Regiments; 1st Bn., 4th and 1st Bn., 8th Regiments (their 2nd Bns. had received colours from the king at the Hague on 7 February).

Battle Losses

The colour of the 2nd/5th Regiment was captured by the British at Veere in Zealand in 1809, and laid up in the Royal Hospital, Chelsea (a replica still hangs there now). All other colours were taken to Paris in 1810 and burned there in January 1814.

The French Period 1810–14:

Eagles of the 1804 pattern were presented to the following Dutch units by the Emperor on 30 June 1811: 2e Lanciers de la Garde Impériale, 3e Grenadiers de la Garde Impériale, 123e, 124e, 126e de Ligne, 33e Léger, 11e Hussards, 14e Cuirassiers, 9e Artillerie. The 125e de Ligne received its 1804 pattern eagle from Count Dumonceau on 2 January 1811 at Amsterdam.

These 1804 pattern eagles were exchanged for the 1811 'tricolour' pattern in May 1812. On 12 April 1811 the two battalions of the 123e de Ligne in Spain were transferred to the 130e de Ligne and new (non-Dutch) battalions were raised for the 123e. The 131e de Ligne was raised in 1812 from the Walcheren Regiment but it is not known if an eagle was presented.

The eagles met the following fates:

2e Lanciers, 3e Grenadiers, 33e Léger: No eagles were taken into Russia, and the 1804 and 1811 pattern colours were handed into Paris, where they were burned in 1814.

123e de Ligne: The returned 1804 pattern eagle was forgotten, and in 1841 was returned to the

French War Ministry; it can now be seen in the Musée de l'Armée. The 1811 colour was saved by Colonel Avizard, hidden by him during his captivity in Russia, but was burnt in 1814 by the reinstated Bourbon monarch. The Regiment had received a new eagle in 1813, but this was captured by the Prussians in January 1814 and placed in the Garrison Church in Potsdam; its present whereabouts is unknown.

124e de Ligne: 1804 eagle stolen from the Musée

Band of the 2nd Bn., 6th Regiment in Hamburg, 1808. The drum-major has a light green tip to his white plume, light blue peripheral feathers and cut-feather hat trim, and silver hat lace; light green facings, silver lace and buttons, crimson and silver bandolier. The three fifers are (left to right) a Voltigeur, with a green sabre strap; a Fusilier, with red and white shako pompon and green, red and white sabre strap; and a Grenadier, with red over white over light blue plume; brass cap plate and scales; white cords; red epaulettes and sabre strap.

Netherlands Infantry Colour, 1815. Obverse: Orange cloth and bow to wreath, green wreath and border leaves; white scroll with gold inscription; blue shield, gold lion with silver sword and arrows, gold bars; brown supporters, gold crown. Gold fringes, cords, tassels, finial; black staff. Reverse: Same borders, the central device being a crowned script 'W' over a unit designation, all in gold. Cavalry standards were the same design but much smaller. After Teupken.

de l'Artillerie by the Prussians in 1815; last known location was the Garrison Church, Potsdam, before World War Two. The 1811 eagle came back safely from Russia and was burnt by royal order after Napoleon's abdication.

125ᵉ de Ligne: 1804 and 1811 eagles—as for 124ᵉ de Ligne.

126ᵉ de Ligne: 1804 eagle as for 123ᵉ; now in the Musée de l'Armée. 1811 eagle captured by the Russians at Borrissow 1812, now in the Summer Palace, Leningrad.

130ᵉ de Ligne: Nothing known.

11ᵉ Hussards: Nothing known.

14ᵉ Cuirassiers: 1804 eagle handed in and burnt in January 1814. 1811 eagle captured at Borrissow 1812 by the Russian Petrograd Dragoons; now in the Summer Palace, Leningrad.

9ᵉ Artillerie: Nothing known.

The 1815 Campaign:
The colours carried in 1815 were orange and bore the royal cypher and the unit designation; the design is shown in detail in the half-tone plate on the left.

The Plates

A1: Jager, 4th Jager Battalion, 1801
The costume shows all the hallmarks of the light troops of the day and also the strong French influence (green plume, epaulettes and sabre knot). Instead of a pack, Jagers had hunting satchels in brown calfskin. The green cords in the bicorn were to hold up the brim and improve the appearance of this unwieldy headgear. After Knötel.

A2: Grenadier, Infantry Regiment Waldeck, 1801
Tunic skirts had become very long in the French fashion since the foundation of the Batavian Republic in 1795, and the turnbacks bore the élite company emblems. The red appointments (plume tip, hat cords, epaulettes and sabre strap) were all after the French fashion, and most of the equipment seems to have been supplied from French magazines. Although the soldiers had now stopped powdering their hair, it was still worn long and in the traditional queue. After Knötel.

A3: Jager of Light Infantry, 1801
Uniform changes came with fair rapidity in this period; one plate by Knötel shows a plain shako with tricolour cockade and green cords and plume, but a watercolour in the Leger and Wapenmuseum, Leiden, of about the same period gives the shako green top and bottom bands, with a black cockade at top left and a green loop extending down to the bottom band where a white button holds it. The plume in the Knötel plate rises from the opposite side of the shako from the cockade. The cuffs on the Legermuseum plate are plain round (Swedish) with white piping and three buttons along the top, and the man has a white top edging to his short, peaked gaiters; he has white belts, and wears no epaulettes. His waistcoat is white, as opposed to the red shown here.

The 2nd ('Red') Lancers of the Garde Impériale, 1810–14. This famous regiment needs no introduction; detailed lists of orders of dress will be found in the Men-at-Arms title *Napoleon's Guard Cavalry*. (J. H. van Papendrecht, courtesy Dutch Army Historical Section)

B1: Trooper, 2nd Cavalry Regiment, 1801

The old-fashioned, large bicorn was still worn at this time; it usually contained an iron ring with cross-pieces over the skull to protect the wearer against sabre cuts, and in action would be worn fore and aft with the plume to the front. As will be seen later, there seem to have been various patterns of saddle furniture in use at this time; the Dragoons have brown fur caps to their holsters, and different lace decoration. The tricolour hat tassels showed the national colour even though the cockade was plain black; the light blue turnbacks were without decoration. The cavalry regiments did not carry carbines. After Knötel.

C1: Officer, 22nd Infantry Battalion, 1803

This battalion was raised for colonial service and went to the Cape of Good Hope, although it would seem that the clothing remained that worn in Holland and must have been very uncomfortable in such a hot climate unless made of very light cloth. The officer's tricolour sash was of interesting design, being held loosely about the waist by a device rather like a modern Boy Scout's 'woggle'—a sphere of about 6cm diameter in red, white and blue with the sash passing through a hole in its centre; the sash terminated in tricolour tassels about eight inches long. Soldiers of this battalion wore the newly introduced stovepipe shako, which apparently did not stand up well to the climate. It is of interest that the sword knot and tassel were plain silver and did not show the national colours. After Knötel.

C2: Officer, 1st Cavalry Regiment, 1804

The undress uniform shown here was worn off

duty and was designed to be an economical alternative to the expensive parade dress. The black and silver bandolier and sword slings were worn in parade dress as well, but it is surprising to see the heavy, old-fashioned boots being worn with this form of dress. The buff breeches were made of leather. After Knötel.

C3: Trooper, 1st Light Dragoons, 1804

In the period 1801–04 several changes of designation, rôle and uniform took place within the cavalry; the 1st Cavalry became the 1st Light Dragoons. The new light dragoons retained the facings of the old regiments, but shortened their coat-tails, and changed the old bicorn for the more dashing 'Tarleton helmet' of the British light dragoons, with its coloured turban, black fur crest and front band with regimental designation. They also retained the straight-bladed sword of their previous service, but the heavy, jacked boots were replaced by shorter, lighter footwear worn under the grey buttoned overalls. After Knötel.

D1: Fusilier Private, Line Infantry, 1801

By comparing various sources, it seems likely that the cockade at this time was black, although Knötel consistently shows the blue-white-red French model. Deduction also leads one to assume that grenadiers had red hat tassels whilst other companies had red, white and blue (fusiliers) or dark green. Note the red musket sling on this and the next figure. The fusiliers carried no sabres; their bayonet sheaths were attached to the pouch bandolier just in front of the pouch, as in the French army.

D2: Karabinier of Light Infantry, 1801

This plate is based on Knötel but modified by documents in the Legermuseum, Leiden, in that the plume has been positioned directly above the cockade (on the left side of the shako) as opposed to Knötel's representation, which shows it on the right. It is of interest that the élite companies seem to have worn short, cut-feather plumes as well as the long, drooping horse-hair type shown here. The white belts are unusual for a light infantry unit.

D3: Private, Centre Companies, 1st Regiment, Dutch Brigade, 1799–1802

As the uniform indicates, this brigade was a foreign formation and was in fact raised by the British from Dutchmen opposed to Napoleon. It had three line infantry regiments and a rifle regiment, and dressed in British-style uniforms with its own identity expressed on cap plates, belt plates and buttons. The cap plate bears the Netherlands' lion and the initials PVO (Prinz von Oranien). Officers had crimson silk waist sashes, and gold and crimson sword knots. Rank badges were as in the British army, as were the inter-company distinctions—red wings trimmed with regimental lace for grenadiers and light companies, white tuft for grenadiers, green for light company. After Knötel, and documents in the Nederlands Legermuseum, Leiden.

Artillery officers, Hamburg, 1808. Both have dark blue coats and breeches; red facings, waistcoats, and piping; gold epaulettes, buttons, lace and sword knot (right), and boot trim (left). The left man has a dark blue plume, the other a red one.

Further studies of the 2nd Bn., 6th Regt. in Hamburg, 1808;
all have red over white over light blue plumes. *Left to right:*
Grenadier with company fanion—white cords, brass plate
and chinscales; red epaulettes, sabre knot and service chevrons; light green facings and fanion lettering. Officer of
Grenadiers—silver cords, epaulette, contre-epaulette, and
crest on gold gorget; gold sword knot; light green facings. On
the right are two Sapeurs of the 3rd Regt. in the old uniform.
Their bearskins are as for the first figure but with crossed
spades on the plate instead of a grenade. They have dark
blue coats with red epaulettes, facings, sabre straps, and
crossed axe arm badges; white buttons; brass decorations
on the white bandoliers.

*E1: Gunner, Horse Artillery, Kingdom of Holland,
1806–10*
This figure is taken from the Augsburger Bilder—
a fairly reliable contemporary source. The hussar
pattern costume was almost universally adopted
at this time for horse artillery, although they very
rarely wore the pelisse.

It is of interest that the shako badge shown here
was worn in 1815, and indeed is still worn today by
the Dutch artillery. According to Lienhart and
Humbert, the horse artillery wore the British-
style Tarleton helmet with a red turban in 1806,
but this was rapidly replaced by the French
pattern shako.

E2: Gunner, Artillery of the Royal Guard, 1806–10
The gold lace to collar and lapels, with their
attendant tassles, indicate guard status, and the
white gaiters show that the summer uniform is
being worn. For everyday wear and for parades
the shako with brass badge and red trim and
plume was worn; the bicorn shown here was
usually reserved for walking out.

E3: Corporal, Dragoons of the Line, 1805
In 1803 this regiment's title was changed from
'Dragoons' to 'Line Dragoons' and on 17 June
1805 it was renamed '1st Dragoons', the existing
1st Light Dragoons became the new 2nd and the
old 2nd was disbanded. The helmet is distinctly of
French pattern, but there is a brass badge on the
front of the brown fur turban. This is only in-
distinctly shown on Suhr's plate of the unit in
Hamburg, but it appears to be a lion's head.

F1: Officer, Jagers of the Guard, 1806–10
This figure is based on an actual uniform pre-
served at the Legermuseum, Leiden. The red top
patch of the bearskin bore a white grenade and
the epaulettes were worn after the French system
of rank badges. On the turnbacks were gold hunting horns; the gold buttons were semi-ball shaped
and quite smooth. The inclining of the lace
buttonholes on the lapels is not mentioned by
readily available sources, which all show these
loops to be horizontal. Other points of interest are
the lack of gold loops on the top two lapel buttons
and the extremely small size of the Polish cuffs.
When taken into the Imperial Guard in 1810 the
Dutch Grenadiers retained their old uniforms but
removed the collar and lapel laces.

F2: Trooper, Chevau-Légers, Belgian Legion, 1814
This whole corps dressed in uniforms apparently
supplied by Austria or at least made up locally to
Austrian patterns, although rank badges seem to
have been French, as Knötel (Volume X, Plate 8,
Uniformenkunde Lose Blätter) shows an infantry
officer with silver sword knot and gold gorget
and epaulette but no waist sash.

The weapons and equipment would almost
certainly have been of French manufacture,
taken over from the disbanded army of the French
province which Holland had become in 1810.

F3: Corporal of Flanquers, Belgian Infantry, 1815
This NCO wears the British shako introduced into that army in 1812 and worn by Belgian infantry units during 1815, with its high front plate probably copied from the headgear worn by the Portuguese army in 1808.

His wooden water canteen is also British pattern and would carry his regimental designation and number in white paint.

While Britain provided much of the equipment used, much else came from appropriated French army stocks such as the sabre and Model 1777 musket shown here. The design of the tape decoration to the dark blue wings worn by the flank companies is peculiar.

G1: Trooper, 6th Dutch Hussars, 1815
Controversy surrounds the exact uniforms worn at Waterloo by the Dutch-Belgian cavalry; Knötel shows the 6th Regiment as being a 'Belgian' regiment on his Plate 37, Volume IV of the *Uniformenkunde Lose Blätter* and this must be a mistake, for

on page 252 of his book *Handbuch der Uniformkunde* he gives the 6th Hussars red facings and the 8th (the real Belgian unit) light blue.

Other sources state that during 1815 both regiments 'wore the same uniform' and Teupken shows both regiments in all light blue dolmans, although this reference is dated later than 1815.

This plate is based purely on actual items displayed in the Legermuseum and shows the details of the black-on-yellow lace on collar and cuffs and the unusual shape of the cuffs themselves.

Officers had red morocco bandoliers and slings decorated with silver and their sabretaches were also in these colours. At Waterloo the 6th and 8th Hussars wore the shako without plumes; the 8th regiment had grey overalls with double red side stripes.

G2: Officer, 5th (Belgian) Light Dragoons, 1815
On his Plate 37, Volume IV of *Uniformenkunde Lose Blätter* Knötel wrongly gives this unit the number '4' (the 4th was a Dutch unit and wore

Dutch infantry skirmishing in the mountains of Spain, 1808–10. The 2nd Regt. are depicted here, with light blue uniform facings. (After J. H. van Papendrecht, courtesy Dutch Army Historical Section)

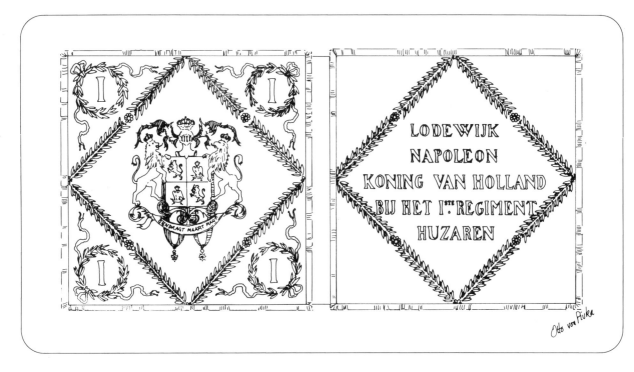

Standard, 1st Hussars 1806–10. Obverse: White centre, sky-blue corners, gold fringes and inscription, sky-blue shield, gold lions and eagles, gold crown and supporters; below the shield a garnet ribbon with black motto 'EENDRAGT MAART MAGT', and below this a red and a sky blue ribbon holding medals. Reverse: White centre, sky-blue corners; gold embroidery, inscriptions and fringes. (Courtesy His Serene Highness Prince Rainier of Monaco)

dark blue tunics faced red with white, hussar-style frogging on the jacket). The 5th Light Dragoons were very similar in dress to the 6th French Chasseurs à Cheval at Waterloo and were indeed mistaken for this unit by their allies during the battle, with tragic consequences. While officers wore the cylindrical shako shown here, other ranks had the bell-topped Austrian model with white top band and lemon-yellow tip to the plume. This unit was originally the Chevau-Légers of the Belgian Legion.

G3: Trumpeter, 2nd (Belgian) Karabiniers, 1815

The three Karabinier regiments wore similar uniforms although there is confusion as to whether the 1st (Dutch) Karabiniers wore the old-fashioned bicorn or the helmet shown here. Trumpeters wore reversed colours as was usual, and the saddle furniture consisted of white sheepskin edged red; a square, dark blue shabraque edged white with white figure '2' diagonally in the rear corner; and an oblong, dark blue porte-manteau with red end piping and white figure '2'. After Knötel.

H1: Lieutenant, Dutch Infantry, 1815

The individual facings originally worn by the infantry battalions in 1814 had probably been discarded by the time of the battle of Waterloo and all wore white as shown here. While many shakos bore the crowned script 'W', the Roman 'W' seems also to have been issued—probably a case of old and new being worn at the same time as often happens, even today. The grey greatcoat was often worn rolled in this fashion when in the field and particularly during a battle, as it provided real protection against sword cuts.

H2: Hornist of Flanquers, 16th (Dutch) Jagers, 1815

To broadcast the commander's orders to light infantrymen on the battlefield it was found that hunting horns were more convenient and effective than the drums used by the Line Infantry. In Dutch units the Austrian-pattern shako was used, while Belgian battalions wore the British Line Infantry shako 1812 pattern, with its extended front plate, immortalized as the 'Waterloo shako' or the Belgic cap.

The shoulder rolls or 'wings' were the badges of flank companies, while the red tuft and the yellow swallow's nests indicated musician status.

H3: National Militiaman 1st Class

Many of the Dutch-Belgian troops at Waterloo were not regulars but rapidly trained militia (not always the best equipped units). All bat-talions wore orange facings and had white turn-backs. The pack and the musket are French; the British wooden water-bottle bore the battalion designation in white: e.g. 'NM/B.No. 7/No. 107'. (National Militia, Battalion No. 7 and the soldier's individual number). The distinctive British light infantry shako is of interest: this is, of course, the felt 'stovepipe' model worn by all British infantry before 1812 and widely distributed to her allies after that date. The usual crowned 'W' appears on the silver sunburst shako plate. There are three silver cuff buttons.

7th Infantry Regt., 1806–10, by van Papendrecht. The regimental colour has a gilt pike tip, gold lettering on the white centre, and red and blue corners. This regiment wore yellow facings, and the musicians yellow coats. (Courtesy Dutch Army Historical Section)

Notes sur les planches en couleur

A1 Uniforme caractéristique des troupes d'infanterie légère—grand emploi du vert—remarquer la sacoche en peau de veau portée en bandoulière et remplaçant le sac à dos. Les cordons verts aident à maintenir le bicorne à large bord en place. **A2** On remarque une forte influence française dans cet uniforme où le soldat portait un fourniment et des armes françaises. **A3** Il existe des contradictions inexpliquées entre une peinture de cet uniforme par Knötel et une autre illustration maintenant au Musée de Leiden.

B Pendant l'action le bicorne était porté d'avant en arrière et non pas en travers de la tête et il couvrait souvent un couvre-chef en fer pour la protection du crâne. Noter les glands tricolores du bicorne. Les basques de la redingote ne portent aucun ornement.

C1 Cette unité fut formée pour servir en Afrique du Sud. Les soldats du régiment portaient le shako en tuyau de poêle nouvellement introduit comme celui illustré à la figure A3. **C2** Il est surprenant de voir ces lourdes bottes de cheval avec un uniforme de tous les jours. **C3** Les changements qui eurent lieu dans l'identité du régiment de 1801 à 1804, donnèrent à cette unité, l'ancien premier régiment de cavalerie, un casque style britannique 'tarleton' au lieu du bicorne et raccourcirent les basques de la redingote.

D1 Voilà encore un air bien français—mais remarquer la bandoulière en cuir rouge des mousquets sur D1 et D2. **D2** Illustration basée sur une peinture de Knötel et des documents du Musée de Leiden. Les ceinturons blancs sont inhabituels pour une unité d'infanterie légère. **D3** Une unité anglaise, vêtue à l'anglaise avec toutes les caractéristiques anglaises évidentes de l'époque.

E1 Cet uniforme est tiré du *Augsburger Bilder*, normalement une source sûre. L'uniforme à la hussard est caractéristique de l'artillerie montée de nombreuses armées de cette époque. On reconnaît la tenue estivale de ville au bicorne et guêtres blanches. Le lacet et les glands dorés sont l'insigne de la garde. **E3** Noter le masque de lion en laiton porté en écusson sur le devant de ce casque à la française.

F1 Illustration d'un uniforme conservé au Musée de Leiden. L'empiècement rouge sur le dessus de ce bonnet en peau d'ours portait une grenade blanche et les revers de la redingote étaient ornés de cors de chasse dorés. **F2** Toute la légion portait des uniformes qui étaient soit fournis par l'Autriche soit confectionnés à partir de patrons autrichiens. **F3** Shako anglais de 1812 et cantine à eau; mousquet et fourniment français.

G1 Plusieurs versions contradictoires de cet uniforme ont été publiées; celle que nous illustrons ici provient du Musée de Leiden. Lacet jaune avec entrelaces noirs. **G2** Uniforme très semblable à celui des 6ᵉ Chasseurs à cheval français et ce régiment fut en fait mépris pour le régiment français à Waterloo entraînant des blessures provoquées par un feu 'ami'. **G3** Ce trompette porte les habituelles couleurs inversées. Il est possible que les 1ers Carabiniers aient porté le bicorne au lieu de ce casque à Waterloo.

H1 Les parements de couleur individuelle des régiments d'infanterie firent place à des parements uniformément blancs en 1814. Le manteau gris enroulé autour de la poitrine offrait une certaine protection contre les coups de sabre. **H2** Toutes les unités hollandaises portaient le shako autrichien en 1815 tandis que les belges portaient le modèle anglais. Le plumet rouge et les ornements jaunes d'épaule identifient un musicien. **H3** Tous les bataillons de la Garde Nationale portaient une veste bleue à parements orange et revers blancs. Le shako en feutre est d'un modèle anglais d'avant 1812; d'autre part ces unités formées en toute vitesse portaient un fourniment et des armes français et anglais mélangés.

Farbtafeln

A1 Typische Uniform der leichtbewaffneten Infanterie der Periode: grüne Farbe in haüfiger Verwendung. Bemerkenswert ist die um den Körper gehängte aus Kalbsleder hergestellte Tasche, die statt dem Rückentornister getragen wurde. Die grünen Leinen dienten zum Aufrechthalten der Krempe des doppelspitzigen Hutes. **A2** Bei dieser Uniform ist ein starker französischer Einfluss bemerkbar, französische Waffen und Ausrüstung wurden getragen. **A3** Zwischen der Abbildung dieser Uniform von Knötel und einer sich heute im Leidener Museum befindenden anderen existieren unerklärte Unterschiede.

B Beim Kampf hatte dieser Reiter seinen doppelspitzigen Hut in länglicher Richtung anstatt quer am Kopf getragen; unter dem Hut würde öfters ein eisernes schädelschützendes Gestell getragen. Zu bemerken sind die Tricolorquasten. Der Rockschoss war ungeziert.

C1 Diese Einheit wurde für den südafrikanischen Dienst ausgehoben. Soldaten des Regiments trugen den neueingeführten 'Angstrohr'-Tschako wie bei A3. **C2** Das Tragen von solchen schweren Reitstiefeln mit dem kleinen Dienstanzug kommt erstaunlich vor. **C3** Mit den Regimentsidentitätsänderungen von 1801–04 wurde dieses Regiment, das 1. Kavallerieregiment, mit einem 'Tarleton'-Helm britischer Art und abgekürztem Rockschoss ausgestattet.

D1 Nochmals ein äusserst französisches Ansehen—zu bemerken sind doch bei D1 und D2 die aus rotem Leder hergestellten Flintentragriemen. **D2** Nach einem Knötelgemälde im Leidener Museum abgebildet. Bei einer leichtbewaffneten Infanterieeinheit kamen solche weisse Gurtriemen selten vor. **D3** Eine von den britischen ausgehobene und britisch angekleidete Einheit, mit offensichtlichen britischen Eigenschaften der Periode.

E1 Diese Uniform is aus den *Augsburger Bilder*—eine gewöhnlicherweise zuverlässige Quelle—entnommen worden. Die husarenartige Uniform war typisch für die reitende Artillerie vieler Heere der Zeit. **E2** Sommerausgangsuniform wie man am doppelspitzigen Hut und den weissen Gamaschen sieht. Eine Einheit der Garde erkennt man durch Goldtresse und Quasten. **E3** Bemerkenswert ist die aus Messing hergestellte Löwenmaske vorne am Helme französischer Art.

F1 Von einer eigentlichen in dem Leidener Museum aufbewahrte Uniform abgebildet. Die rote Tuchabzeichen oben am Bärenfellmütze war mit einer weissen Granate geschmückt und goldene Jagdhörner wurden auf den Rockaufschlägen angebracht. **F2** Die ganze belgische Legion trug Uniforme entweder aus Oesterreich geliefert oder an Ort und Stelle nach oesterreichischem Muster hergestellt. **F3** Britische 1812-Tschako und Feldwasserflasche, französische Flinte und Ausrüstungen.

G1 Verschiedene sich widersprechende Ausführungen dieser Uniform sind herausgegeben worden: unsere Abbildung ist nach Einzelheiten dargestellt worden, die im Leidener Museum aufbewahrt sind. Die Tresse ist gelb mit eingewobenem schwarzem Zickzackmuster. **G2** Die Uniform ist der der französischen 6ᵉ Chasseurs à Cheval sehr ähnlich und bei der Waterlooschlacht wurde dieses Regiment tatsächlich irrtümlich für das französische Regiment genommen und dabei wurden Verluste durch 'freundliches' Feuer verursacht. **G3** Dieser Trompeter trägt die üblichen umgekehrten Farben. Es ist möglich, dass die 1. Karabiniere bei der Waterlooschlacht den doppelspitzigen Hut anstatt des hier geschilderten Helmes getragen haben.

H1 Einzelne Aufschlagfarben der Infanterieregimente sind im Jahre 1814 auf weiss umgeändert worden. Der graue, zusammengerollte Wintermantel diente einigermassen zum Schutz gegen Säbelhiebe. **H2** Im Jahre 1815 trugen alle holländische Einheiten den oesterreichischen Tschako während die Belgier das britische Modell trugen. Der rote Federbusch und gelbe Schulterverzierung bezeichnen einen Musiker. **H3** Alle Milizbataillonen trugen blaue Röcke mit orangegelben Aufschlägen und weissen Rockumschlägen. Der Tschako ist das aus Filz hergestellte vor-1812 Modell; diese rasch ausgehobene Einheiten trugen einen Gemisch von französischen und britischen Waffen und Ausrüstungen.